Hollywood
When Silents Were Golden

Howe Library
Shenandoah College
and
Conservatory of Music

Presented by

Mr. James McNally

Hollywood
WHEN SILENTS WERE GOLDEN

Evelyn F. Scott

MABEL NORMAND

McGraw-Hill Book Company

NEW YORK ST. LOUIS SAN FRANCISCO
DÜSSELDORF LONDON MEXICO SYDNEY TORONTO

DESIGN: HERB JOHNSON
ART DIRECTOR: HARRIS LEWINE

Copyright © 1972 by Evelyn F. Scott
All rights reserved. Printed in the United States of America. No part of this publication may be reproduced, stored in a retrieval system, or transmitted, in any form or by any means, electronic, mechanical, photocopying, recording, or otherwise, without the prior written permission of the publisher.

FIRST EDITION

Scott, Evelyn F.
  Hollywood when silents were golden.
  1. Dix, Beulah Marie, 1876–   2. Moving-picture Industry—Hollywood, Calif.—History.   I. Title.
PS3507.I9Z87   791.43'09794'94   72-37361
ISBN: 0-07-055802-7

```
PS        Scott, Evelyn F.
3507
.19       Hollywood when silents
Z87           were golden
1972
791.4309 Sco83h
```

WITH LOVE FOR
Beulah Marie Dix
AND
George M. Flebbe

Contents

1.	HOLLYWOOD PRE-HOLLYWOOD	1
2.	ARRIVING	6
3.	A DAY WITH JOAN OF ARC	10
4.	BEULAH MARIE DIX: AUTHOR	15
5.	THE GOLD AND SILVER SPIDER	21
6.	ACTING	28
7.	MOVIES IN THE MOUNTAINS	33
8.	BEULAH MARIE DIX: PLAYWRIGHT	39
9.	BEULAH MARIE DIX: SCREENWRITER— ON THE LOT	47
10.	HOLLYWOOD FOUR SIX	53
11.	SCHOOL SETS IN	61
12.	BEULAH MARIE DIX: ORIGINAL STORY AND CONTINUITY	68
13.	FAMOUS BOYS	74
14.	SWIMMING POOLS I HAVE KNOWN	80
15.	ON A CLEAR DAY YOU CAN SEE HAYAKAWA	88

Contents

16.	BEING BAD	95
17.	PARADISE	102
18.	FLY WITH HARRY HOUDINI	107
19.	THE MONTESSORI CLASS	114
20.	MOTHER MEETS THE CENSORS	120
21.	PARTIES I	127
22.	BACKGROUND MUSIC	134
23.	FAMOUS GIRL	142
24.	UNDER THE PICKLE SIGN	149
25.	SET-WATCHING	156
26.	DRESS AND UNDRESS	163
27.	BLUE IS THE NIGHT	170
28.	UP AT THE HOUSE	176
29.	SHOULDER-RUBBING, AND OTHER TALES	182
30.	COME WITH ME WHERE MOONBEAMS	190
31.	PARTIES II	197
32.	LEAVING	205
33.	HOLLYWOOD, FRANCE	211
34.	S.W.A.K.	217
35.	LATER	221

Hollywood
When Silents Were Golden

I
Hollywood Pre-Hollywood

Once upon a time a small town was created on the ocean side of Los Angeles by a couple from the Middle West. They selected a nice swatch of land at the hemline of the hills, and they named it Hollywood.

There wasn't any holly in Hollywood. The English holly bushes they imported quickly died. But the seed of make-believe they had sown was to bear much fruit around the world.

The first development of Hollywood, from 1886 to 1910, was rather slow and probably not stimulating to anybody but an orange-watcher. Hollywood's great crops were pineapples, lemons, winter cucumbers, and refugees from Eastern cold who counted on the climate to prolong their middle age.

Hollywood's population, circa 1907, reached almost three thousand, in nine hundred homes. Most homes turned their backs on foothill canyons where, it was claimed, roué Angelenos perched their Love Nests. Hollywood, which critics soon would claim was one Super–Love Nest, had no vice. Guests at the Hollywood Hotel might lounge on the veranda, but not with glass in hand. The hotel was minus liquor license. Hollywood had no crime. An occasional wrongdoer spent a night locked up in the town marshal's extra room, for there was no jail.

In a *respectable* canyon back of the Hollywood Hotel, Carrie Jacobs Bond most suitably set down her song "A Perfect Day."

Hollywood When Silents Were Golden

That was before the movies came.

Who would have expected quiet little Hollywood to be transformed by a business that had only just begun, several thousand miles away?

Movies as major entertainment, not experiments or peep shows, really started in 1903 on the East Coast with *The Great Train Robbery*, a landmark because it was a film that told a story. By 1907 half-a-dozen companies were at work turning out one-reel motion pictures, from New Jersey to Chicago. These pictures didn't cost much, but even modest financing was not easy to find. How could you have confidence in a budget that depended on how long the sun stayed out? Artificial lighting hadn't advanced far enough to give much help.

Colonel Selig, making movies in Chicago, sent the first scout for a survey of the sunshine of the West. To the halloo of the coyotes in the Hollywood Hills was presently added a new cry which grew to be almost as indigenous: "Action! Camera!"

The movies actually moved first into Los Angeles. The Selig and Lubin Companies settled down in 1908, not far from the City Hall. Other studios scattered into quarters north and south. Yet they all seemed restless, whether in the civic center or far out with the dry farming and the orange groves. Then David Horsley leased an empty tavern in little Hollywood, in 1911. It was a good compromise. His competitors crowded round. Hollywood, the motion-picture capital, was born.

Hollywood, in fact, had been incorporated into Los Angeles by then, but its chief tie was the Big Red Cars and its individuality was strong. Hollywood, and not Los Angeles, became the synonym for movies.

In 1911 Hollywood was still quite small. Its houses had climbed only halfway up the hills which they would ultimately dot from foot to top. There was a wilderness for motion-picture use anywhere you raised your eyes. There were big bungalows and minor mansions, too, for further background, but Hollywood Boulevard—apart from the Hollywood Hotel—had few distinctive edifices. Grauman's Chinese Theatre, with its fore-

Hollywood Pre-Hollywood

court full of famous movie foot- and handprints, was still fifteen years away. The sidewalks had no inlaid stars. Hollywood Boulevard could double on the screen for almost any home town street.

In Hollywood the movies throve. They fattened from one reel to two, or four, or six. Instead of costing a mere few thousand dollars, a "special" might cost as much as a hundred thousand, a great deal by the standards of five years before and nothing compared with the millions of the 1950s. Actors in an early comedy once pooled their petty cash to meet expenses and complete the film. By 1915 actor Charlie Chaplin earned a salary of twelve hundred and fifty dollars per week, and eighteen thousand theatres were waiting to repay the studio investment at a profit, even with admissions of a quarter or ten cents.

In 1917 motion pictures rated as Southern California's largest single industry. They employed twenty thousand people and released thirty million dollars back to the economy. Even then, Hollywood had not changed much. Most Hollywoodians went about their tasks in offices and shops as before. The difference was that the drive or walk to work might be interrupted by a movie chase or that your neighbor at the weekly sing could be a star. Next week, for that matter, *you* could be a star.

For a while, at least, that's how it seemed. The outside world believed it and began to act on it quite soon, with waves of emigration that were for the most part going to ebb in disillusionment. There seemed to be such an insatiable, no doubt endless, appetite for movies at the box office, and so the studios all had an insatiable appetite for stars. Universal Studio alone kept sixteen companies at work making pictures while there was daylight six days of the week. That meant room for quite a few performers. Sometimes the only acting qualification needed was to be on hand and to be good-looking. This might lead to a career of several dozen roles, over a period of several years, which then sank without a trace.

The public soon demanded more of its idols than a body that moved and a marcel that didn't. Some producers demanded

more from the start. Down the road a lemon toss from Horsley's Tavern, Jesse Lasky, Samuel Goldfish (later Goldwyn), and Cecil de Mille formed the Lasky Company, in 1914, in a barn. They had exposure to the theatre in New York and they believed in New York quality. They induced stage performers Dustin Farnum, Fannie Ward, and even Geraldine Farrar from the opera, to try the West. The Lasky Company eventually became Famous Players–Lasky, emphasizing talent.

The Famous Players of those days have been forgotten now almost as completely as the amateurs. To try to piece their movie pasts together is a bit like reconstructing prehistoric creatures from the fossil fragments in our asphalt pits. Just a few names from those years have meaning now. Dustin Farnum is recalled, thanks to a young actor of the 1970s, named Dustin for him. There are also Chaplin, Pickford, Fairbanks, and directors Griffith and de Mille—whose pictures still are often shown, whose impact stays.

It has been a fashion for motion-picture buffs to set Griffith and a few others on pinnacles much higher than de Mille—Griffith for *The Birth of a Nation* and the close-up; Thomas Ince for innovations like his antiwar picture *Civilization* and the unique idea of writing motion-picture stories down; Mack Sennett for his special comedy approach. Cecil de Mille is assigned a hummock further down.

Yet for forty years, glorifying the bathtub and the Bible, among other things, Cecil de Mille went on directing popular movies when his peers were gone. Whether with religious exhortation, pagan revel, rugged grandeur, or exotic plumbing, he became a household word. If he didn't reach the Everest of art, he established a plateau for an industry.

On the edge of this plateau, Beulah Marie Dix, novelist and playwright of moderate success (and my mother), set foot with me in the summer of 1916. We came West to visit Cecil de Mille's mother. Movies were not our concern. At the age of five, I knew nothing about movies. At the age of forty, Mother thought she

Hollywood Pre-Hollywood

knew too much—they were something fathered on the magic lantern by burlesque! If anyone had told her that she was to stay through the next three decades, writing for the movies, and that I would go to school in Hollywood instead of Boston, she probably would have packed us back aboard the next Eastbound train.

We were going, nonetheless, to be a part of Hollywood until the 1930s, till the talkies, the Depression, World War II, and finally (perhaps very finally) television made "our" movies change. Our associates would be film directors, writers, actors, cutters, and designers. Some of our best friends were to be Goldwyns and de Milles.

The years from 1916 to 1930 were, for me, the years from five to nineteen when you believe that right there, in your sneakers or your pumps, you are immortal. Those were the years when Hollywood appeared immortal, too. Now nobody seems quite so sure. But growing up in Hollywood was very good, when Hollywood was growing up.

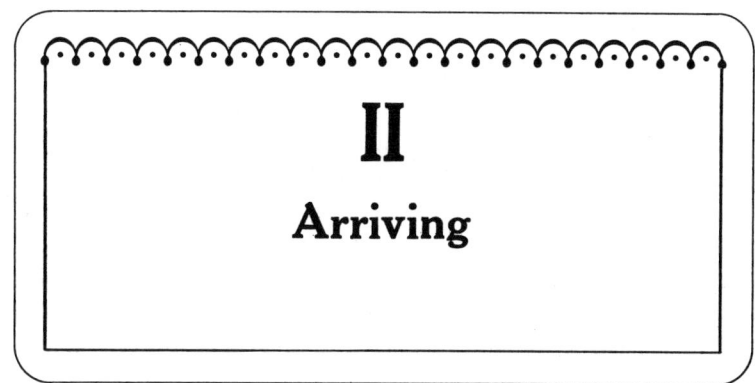

II
Arriving

We arrived on July 2, 1916—wonderful weather, just as advertised. Neither we nor it were newsworthy. Otherwise, the *Los Angeles Times* of that date was as full of news as a pterodactyl egg of meat.

In France, the Battle of the Somme had begun to rage.

In Chesapeake Bay, a German submarine was lurking, on reliable report.

In Washington, D.C., President Wilson was exchanging notes with Mexican President Carranza. Wilson's notes, the *Times* seemed to think, were pretty mild. A cartoon portrayed him as a stenographer typing away, while Uncle Sam, in battle dress, glared at him. The caption was "The girl he left behind."

In Los Angeles, the Mexican crisis was occasioning some agitation for a Home Guard (the National Guard had been posted to the Border) in case of an uprising by some of the Mexican-background local population. In addition, there was the problem of a longshoremen's strike down at the port, but it had not prevented two thousand pleasure seekers from taking boats to offshore Catalina Island on the day before. For those who didn't wish to go to sea, Thomas Ince was sponsoring a benefit rodeo, at the beach.

Inside Los Angeles, entertainment ranged from Anna Pavlova dancing her renowned *Dying Swan* to Charlie Chaplin on

Arriving

the screen in *The Fireman*, or Dustin Farnum in *The Lightning Conductor*, with Hunter's Posing Dogs live, on-stage.

A rose—the world's loveliest, of course—had just been christened for Los Angeles, though that week not everything about the city had been roses. Eight divorce suits were filed; in a single day, motorcars had snuffed out two among some half a million lives. To be fair, though, not only motorcars had accidents. Up in Oakland, an explosion damaged the smoking car of a train just as it pulled in. Someone's luggage had concealed a bomb!

Nothing like that threatened us. Our only hazard on arriving at the station was climbing down the Pullman steps. Mother and I both had short legs, she by constitution, I by age. We were oval-shaped. Otherwise we didn't look alike. Mother's hair was brown. Mine was red, as a result of her earnest prayers. Her nose was long; mine was snub. She was beginning to wonder if she should have prayed more about that.

We got off the train at Pasadena, not Los Angeles a few miles farther on, because our hostess wished to take us out to Hollywood by "the pretty way," not the ugly one from the main depot.

She was waiting underneath a palm tree. She had hair that looked like hammered silver, and seemed pretty old. Almost everybody that I met seemed old. Mother hadn't married till past thirty. I already knew that our hostess had two children Mother's age, William and Cecil. Her name was Beatrice de Mille, and we were to call her Bibi.

After her hair, I noticed her black eyes, tinged with gold, which were like the strongest coffee coming to a boil. She wore a trailing dress, beads, combs, a scarf, and, for driving, a green veil. She had brought a car borrowed from her son Cecil, since her own wasn't large enough for us and the hand luggage needed on a five-day trip. A chauffeur stowed us in, and we were swung away from the station, which, architecturally, with its tiles and arches, was a cousin of the nearby Green Hotel.

Hollywood When Silents Were Golden

As we drove across a bridge which had no water underneath it, Bibi and Mother talked about "the boys," William and Cecil, who had come to Southern California to make movies. Bibi had followed them and then invited Mother, whom she knew In The Theatre in New York, to pay her a visit. Bibi had been New York agent for some of Mother's plays.

Back in Boston, Mother had despised the movies. Nickelodeons! They were trashy, in a class with comic strips. She had come West to see the country and a friend, but she was courteous, of course, and if this friend could truly be engrossed in films—Bibi, it seemed, was even writing motion-picture plays—then there had to be a little more to them than flash-and-smash.

I don't suppose I listened. I was nearly stupefied—ten more miles of view! A golf course was the only stretch of "back East" green. Bibi bought some grapefruit from a roadside stand. The price seemed a happy shock to Mother.

Then we were in Hollywood, and Bibi had us driven along Hollywood Boulevard because we would do our errands there, not because it was a streak of light and glamour right across the vision of the world. She took us also past the Lasky Studio, where she and "the boys" worked. It was silvery grey and, like her, it had a veil, a green haze of pepper trees.

Halfway up a hill, we came to Bibi's house. It was a bungalow, not the little and white kind, but big and brown, two stories, with a roof line that sagged, looking Japanese. It sat on a high foundation that enclosed a basement with a furnace which would spare us Southern California's first bitter disappointment: *why, it's cold at night—outside you need a coat and inside you need heat!*

Fifteen steps led to a porch under ivy, ivy with rounded leaves, not the cornered kind we had at home. Suddenly I missed my home, the wet smell of the woods, the lady's-slippers you might find (but never pick) while walking to our cousins' farm, Pullaway (my rocking horse), and my father, who had had to stay in his bookstore selling books.

Arriving

I missed home less, once I was inside Bibi's house. There was a blue rug, different from any others I had seen—Chinese—lots of benches, shelves, and even a desk, all built in, of auburn wood, an incense burner shaped like a volcano, puffing pleasant-smelling smoke, and an "altar rail" around the fireplace. This proved to be a perfect place for me to sit, though it was meant for grown-up feet.

Back across the porch you could see the hills. *Lion-colored hills*, my mother said, and then corrected, *cougar-colored hills*, as better suited to the West. On the skyline just across from us ran Vine Street, to the Boulevard and to Bibi's (and the boys') studio.

Bibi called us on into the dining room. This was a good room, too. It had a cabinet, carved and inlaid with niches and drawers and the minutest bridge. It had a sideboard ornamented with a bronze lady on a bronze horse. In spite of her unlikely clothes and the falcon on her wrist, I took her to be Bibi, flanked by William and Cecil, also in bronze, as her guards. There was also a table with a mirror in the center and a circle of flower vases clasped by crystal chains.

Most wonderful of all, if you stepped on a panel in the floor, a door slid wide. *Sesame!* What magic might not lie beyond?

In warm fact, nothing but the kitchen. The panel was a device to help a maid with trays. But I didn't stay awake for facts. Bibi took us to our downstairs bedroom and I fell asleep while Mother was wondering if she could smell the ocean as well as incense, oil, and sage and oranges in the glowing air. Tomorrow, I dreamed, if I stamped hard and said *Sesame!*, I would walk through a sliding door into all the treasures of a California Ali Baba's cave.

III

A Day with Joan of Arc

Good weather $\times$ scenic splendor $+$ distance $=$ Southern California, and no Southern Californian of even recent status failed to take advantage of all three. We were planning to stay with Bibi three or four weeks, but she wasn't wasting any of it.

Next morning, in the gleaming heat, we went over what Mother termed a mountain pass but was just a foothill notch into the San Fernando Valley and the Duchy of Lorraine. I had a picture book about the life of Joan of Arc, so I knew Lorraine was where that brave heroine had lived. Out in the Valley, Cecil de Mille was shooting scenes for a movie about Joan of Arc.

We were driven in the big car again. This time Cecil de Mille's wife, Constance, came along, but her two children did not. I was to call her Aunt Constance. It would be another ten years before younger people daringly addressed their elders by first names. Meanwhile, rather than say *Mrs.* and *Mr.* to close family friends, those of us under twenty found ourselves with droves of "courtesy" uncles and aunts.

Aunt Constance was very calm and quiet, all the years we were to know her—just a bit preoccupied. When she spoke, she hesitated slightly, a habit which I loved, perhaps because a child would only hear friendly things from her: she never was unkind. She was beautiful, as well. A story widely circulated

A Day with Joan of Arc

in her family was that Cecil de Mille made up his mind to marry her just on glimpsing her legs. At the age of five, I took small note of beauty in mothers. Mothers stood apart from consideration of mere looks; furthermore, *standing*, or hurrying to offer aid, was the only reason they had legs.

After leaving Cahuenga Pass on the historic road used by the Mission Fathers in the early days, we descended to the flats and passed a little brood of buildings hatched out among weeds. Universal City, Bibi told us, *another* studio. Every studio seemed to be completely separate. Universal, Lasky, Ince, or Fine Arts people kept apart, to some extent because of long hours and long distances, but also because the intense competition of a new business, where a small fortune might be won and a large one lost, required constant invention and encouraged secrecy.

Aunt Constance warned us to tell no one what the subject of her husband's present picture was. When word had got round the year before that he was making *Carmen*, someone else rushed through a version of the story on the theory that the public would buy tickets to whichever came out first. Cecil de Mille wasn't yet a name that on its own could guarantee a long line at the box office.

In the flats it was very hot. What air there was seemed clogged with groves of oranges and peaches, plus a billboard or two. There was even a mirage—what looked like a shallow puddle—shining on the surface of the road, always a few feet beyond the car. When we got to Domremy, Joan of Arc's village, we found a well, but it too was a sham, and a dreadful disappointment to a thirsty child.

Mother was in ecstasy. What sham! Used to the one-sidedness of sets for the stage, she was entranced by the almost perfect "stone" and half-timbered cottages facing on the village square. The buildings had at least three sides, for the camera would view them from more angles than could any theatre audience. They were built against the hills in such a

11

way that only trees would be in view—no cactus, which is not common to Lorraine.

Trained pigeons fluttered round the village belfry. There was a baby—not so trained. It cried. There were dogs and chickens and pigs. On a platform commanding people, animals, France, and, to my mind, all of history, stood Cecil de Mille. I looked up at him and made my "knicks," a half-curtsy which soon, luckily, succumbed to the crudeness of the West.

Uncle Cecil de Mille had a brisk, controlled face, a bright smile, and Bibi's eyes. He was wearing khaki and puttees. I already wished we had puttees. The California brush, bristling round except inside the village square, stabbed where it didn't slash. Foxtails poked into my socks and between my shoelaces. I felt full of pins, but this was no time to complain; the flight of villagers from the invaders was going to begin.

Joan the Woman was part modern, as were all of Uncle Cecil's pictures then. Historic grandeur got confined to flashbacks. In this case the flashback overwhelmed the modern story, displaying most of the life of Joan of Arc as envisioned by a World War I soldier, Wallie Reid, who decided in the trenches that he had fought with her in that other war.

Wallie Reid, then considered the handsomest young actor on the screen, didn't take part in the flight from Domremy. Geraldine Farrar was in the thick of it, as Joan. She was handsome, too. She had fine features, a proud carriage, and black hair. She was one of the leading opera singers of the day, and already had had movie success, starring in Uncle Cecil's *Carmen*, her most famous opera role, though of course in the picture not a sound came from her mouth.

Geraldine Farrar was a native diva, born in Boston, with a debut in Berlin. Singers went to Europe to be taken seriously, then. There was a rumor—which I heard a great deal later—that the German Crown Prince took her seriously indeed, absolutely captivated.

A Day with Joan of Arc

Bibi pointed out this doubly-shining star for me. Geraldine Farrar was wearing a black bodice and a brown skirt like any other female villager, but once you recognized her you saw no one else. Just as in one of Mother's favorite quotations, "where the MacGregor sat was always head of the table," so where Farrar set foot was center stage. In the drawings I had seen of Joan of Arc, the heroine was sandy haired, slender, with a fearless look, and very young. Brunette Geraldine Farrar was not exactly slender or quite young. Fearless? We should see.

When the scene began, the noise dropped off—not, of course, because the camera could hear, but because the actors needed to. There were a hundred or so, a throng for those days, waiting for directions. The cameras—two, I think—began to turn. The alarming enemy (Burgundians), in metal helmets and chain mail, brawled down the slope. The pigeons wheeled. The villagers began to run, carrying whatever could be snatched from their cottages. Mother had observed already, with a dramatist's envy, the variety of splendid props—coffers, basins, tankards, coverlets.

In the forefront of the action, a comfortably stout actress, Lillian Leighton, swept up a piglet and a goose. As she headed down the village street, there was trouble with the little pig. It squirmed and shrieked, enough to risk disrupting the scene and drowning out commands. All at once Farrar was at her side, seized the pig, smacked it, and tucked it underneath her arm, where it remained in apparently shocked silence as she went on with the flight. The scene ended as rehearsed; it was a good "take."

Mother had fallen silent as the pig. Not because Farrar, the diva, had been so quick-witted and so deft, but because Farrar, the Boston Irishwoman, hadn't hesitated, despite hoary anti-Irish jokes, to be capable about a pig. This Joan, too, was fearless.

In the car on our way home we hardly spoke. I itched

from foxtails, but my spirit soared, with Farrar and the little pig. Mother's mind must have turned more to Uncle Cecil, for she wrote her mother in New England that night, *I have more respect for the motion picture world than I ever thought to have, but as yet I see no chance in it for the author.*

Generations of writers, frenzied at what movies would do to their stories, would agree.

IV

Beulah Marie Dix: Author

Mother was an author.

At the turn of the century, when she began to write for a living, quite a lot of women wrote. Two of them were at the head of the Best Seller list of 1900. Mother never reached the list, but she had twenty-eight books in print between 1899 and 1941. Her juvenile *Merrylips* was recommended reading at the public libraries for decades.

America's favorite fiction in the 1890s and the early 1900s was historical romance. All Mother's early books qualified. They were romantic in the sense of swashbuckling, never sugary, and they were historically exact. Mother was serious about research, which she felt many of her peers of either sex were not. Possets, poignards, or pomander boxes were not wrongly set in a page she wrote. Even in *Merrylips*, she made sharply clear that warfare hurt—unexpected honesty in a book for ten-year-olds at the heyday of literary derring-do.

Mother *was* serious. Life never seemed light-hearted in New England, with all those traditions and those draughts; besides, she had her special problems.

She was born in Kingston, Massachusetts, in what she referred to as the Centennial Year. Eighty years afterwards, asked to specify which Centennial, she replied, "Why, of the United States, of course." What other centennial could there be? The anniversary of the founding of her country still felt

close in the 1870s. In New England it absolutely nudged. While the branches of her family tree were not thick with heroes, one ancestor did do his part in the first sea fight of the Revolution and her sister's husband was descended from the first man hanged in the Plymouth Colony. He was very proud of it. A gallows ten feet high is hard to top.

Kingston became part of Plymouth, but Mother never really lived in Plymouth much, physically or in her imaginings. Her parents moved away when she was small. *Soldier Rigdale*, a children's book about the Plymouth Colony, which she wrote on assignment, she considered dull, and *A Rose O' Plymouth Town* was to me the least exciting of her plays. Plymouth (Kingston) got even by burning up her birth certificate in a city fire, though I think she was glad of this because a midwife put her down in the records ignominiously as "Baby Girl Dix."

As a child, I thought that what her parents christened her—Beulah Marie!—was little better. Beulah, she explained, was the Biblical Land of Promise. Her parents had emerged from troubled times, loss of a child, and life on a frontier (St. Louis), when she made her arrival on Cape Cod. So they called her Beulah, with the addition of Marie, then the fashionable form for Maria, which was her mother's name. At least, she always said, you couldn't forget it—which was true. What she had really wanted, though, was to have been a boy called Tommy Drew.

She laughed later at what psychiatrists might make of this. In Chelsea and Lynn, near Boston, where she grew up, she played with dolls, but not maternally. She put her dolls through grueling dramatic scenes inspired by the books available—the Bible, Longfellow, Dickens, *Border Ballads*. Bored to the teeth by what was then thought properly female— primping, nattering, and petticoats—she began to write the adventures she would have liked to have as Tom.

Perhaps she oversimplified. Disliking so many girlish things,

she assumed the opposites were indigenous to boys. Boys were, therefore, gallant, steadfast, absolutely honest, loyal to a fault, indomitably brave. It took time for her to understand that such qualities were not merely rare in women, but rare. It took time and experience to distinguish them, and at last she found them just as much in women as in men, and made lifelong friends of both. Bibi would be one.

In school, not surprisingly, she was much alone. She was always the youngest in her class, brilliant, and not long on tact. Tact was not quite honest. She continued playing with dolls (drilling them in Shakespeare) when she was at Chelsea High School and her girl classmates started doing up their hair. Hair was one of Mother's problems. She could never manage hers. It kinked, it would stay short, and no matter how she tugged it back into a knot, strands escaped to cause a little haze around the strong lines of her long-nosed, earnest face. She had a high color, too—cheerful rosy cheeks which, added to a figure measuring 36-30-36 by the time she was fourteen, further interfered with images of Tommy Drew.

At sixteen she entered Radcliffe, which was still Harvard Annex. Not a great many women went to college in the 1890s. What for? Few careers would be open to them at the end of four expensive years. Henry Dix, a factory foreman, scarcely could afford them, but he took pride in his daughter's grades—all A's except when Math crept in—and he wished her to have her chance. She considered her tuition as a loan to repay as soon as she began to teach. She would teach, of course. That was the respectable and logical result of a degree. Her sense of obligation was especially acute since her older sister Christine would not get equal opportunity.

Mother always thought my Aunt Chris would have been a business whizz. She could cook up a storm, and she was a first-rate organizer of raffles and bazaars. However, there and then, business was an evil word in connection with a woman.

All the family had felt besmirched when my grandmother's sister, in her widowhood, took an office job to support herself and her small child, rather than become a family charge, perhaps divided to two different homes. What matter that her office was a government bureau in the nation's capital? What matter that Jessie Soule turned out so competent she was issued the department's first typewriter, awe-inspiring as a motorcar and looming nearly half as big! It wasn't *nice*. No wonder her child grew up to go on the stage.

Mother's sister Christine grew up to wrestle with a water pump, a cesspool, a corn patch, canning, washing in a tub, sewing everything she wore on a treadle machine, freezing and sweating, and all those *nice* things you do on a tiny, failing farm.

If Baby Beulah had represented a Promised Land to Henry and Maria Dix in 1876, Radcliffe represented one to Beulah in 1893. The people she had known till then were literate, but they were occupied with the things they felt came first: coal, custard, church. Mother hated household chores—keeping the oil lamps clean (her particular job) or helping to cook. She was relieved of cooking when one day she beat the bottom from a bowl while she was thinking about *Scottish Chiefs*. Church, she didn't mind; she had a deep and tolerant faith. The Bible was literature, besides.

At Radcliffe, thanks to a free-elective system where nothing she considered humdrum was required, except gym, literature could always come first. Radcliffe swarmed with individuals as addicted to books, as in love with history, as obsessed with drama, as was she. Her enlarged vocabulary—any word she found, she used, and she found a lot of words—was accepted readily, not giggled at. Her emphatic ways were no surprise. Radcliffe women as a whole were far from vacuous. Most of the members of her class joined it with ambition, and at a sacrifice.

Of course there were others, too—rich girls who, she

Beulah Marie Dix: Author

thought, "took" Radcliffe in the place of another European tour. She had nothing against them and their pretty clothes, but she never got acquainted with them, either. Gertrude Stein, a special student and a presence even then, was, because of wealth, just about invisible to Mother's eyes. She did remember Gertrude when in due course the world was faced with the surprising Stein statement, "A rose is a rose is a rose," but she wasn't impressed. Years later, though, she *was* impressed by Gertrude Stein's *Four Saints in Three Acts*, and another phrase, "Pigeons in the grass alas." She could hear the lutes and cymbals in this.

Mother got a lot from Radcliffe. Not so much, she decided afterwards, from the writing classes—she began to doubt if writing could be taught—but from English and history. For fifty years her face would light up as she spoke of Dr. Kittredge, the authority on Chaucer and Shakespeare. She also studied Dante, French classics, and some Anglo-Saxon, and she wrote plays in which she acted, usually as a boy. Radcliffe gave Tommy Drew his finest years.

Mother's plays in her college years took place in the seventeenth century—for a long time her home away from home. Her first heroine on the Radcliffe stage was played by her small, pretty classmate Josephine Sherwood. Josephine looked bewitching in the Puritan clothes. For a while it seemed as though she would have to use that witchery to hold the stage alone. Radcliffe dignitaries decreed that trousers must not be worn by young women cast as boys. There was a revolt, not, of course, with bricks. Burning with conviction, these students glowed with dignity, too; till they knew each other very well, they called each other *Miss*. The revolt was settled with a compromise—gym bloomers. Mother tried to make her acting yet more Tommy Drew, to offset the bloomers with the pink cheeks and the fuzzy hair.

After graduation, Josephine Sherwood married a promising young actor, Shelley Hull, and, as Josephine Hull, crowned a

lengthy Broadway career with famous roles in *You Can't Take It With You*, *Arsenic and Old Lace*, and *Harvey*. Mother, however, thought that Josephine undertook her greatest role when she was still a bride. The groom obtained a stock contract in the Middle West, a job the young Hulls needed very much. Stock companies counted, for a part of their receipts, on the yearnings of the female audience towards their leading men. Yearnings in the early 1900s in the Middle West had their moral code. Leading men were expected to be bachelors.

The bride and groom could not face months apart, so Josephine went West as Shelley's sister. She needed all her art to remain a graceful fixture in the background, while his admirers, in the words Mother used back then, "batted their eyes at him."

Mother ended her undergraduate years in 1897, at the age of twenty, summa cum laude, Phi Beta Kappa, and the first woman to win Harvard's Sohier literary prize. She went on to get her Master's degree, but she never taught. She sold a story written when she was eighteen. With the ten-dollar check she bought a coat she wore ten years. Obviously she could make more money writing than teaching. It was even respectable. Best of all, it was what she wished to do.

V

The Gold and Silver Spider

Because she came to Hollywood as an author, and especially as an author-friend of Bibi's, who back in New York had practically launched Edward Knoblock (*Kismet*) and promoted Avery Hopwood (*The Bat*), Mother was socially a mini-lioness.

Constance de Mille gave a luncheon for her. Anna, William de Mille's wife, gave a tea. Teas were important coeducational events to which Anna was prone. One of her many interesting guests of honor was Count Tolstoi, the great writer's son, whom Mother dismissed as an amiable enthusiast. He knew all about the Russia of the moment, from a spot nine thousand miles away! An unseen guest at every Anna de Mille gathering was her father, Henry George, who had been the father of Single Tax as well. Mother felt he had been a great man all right, but did he have to turn up in all conversations like (one of her favorite quotations from Dickens) King Charles' head?

Marie Doro and her husband, Elliott Dexter, who were Lasky stars, entertained with dinner. It was usual then for women to play boys' parts on the stage—boys had a disrupting tendency to grow, or even let their voices change, during the prolonged run of a play. Marie Doro was repeating the title role of her great stage hit, *Oliver Twist*, for the screen. Earlier she had been woven into Mother's woof by appearing on Broadway in a play with Shelley Hull.

I like the people out here, Mother wrote East. *There is a*

reality about the motion picture work that seems to knock some of the staginess out of them. Or is it perhaps that Eastern people out here are particularly cordial to each other?

Did we Easterners "from the theatre" tend to huddle for warmth in a hostile atmosphere? I was not aware of being a tenderfoot or an intruder, but I could sense that the foothills, which were only added back yard or location during the day, became vast and primitive at night.

However that may have been, if Bibi was too busy to go shopping with Mother, or to drive to the Valley or the beach, someone else of her group would go, perhaps Veda Buckland, whose husband, the Belasco set designer, had created Domremy and later would build the superb castle for Douglas Fairbanks' *Robin Hood*.

To me, shopping in Los Angeles was fairly dull. My favorite landmark, except for the Pig'n Whistle, was a marble statue rising strangely in the center of Robinson's department store. The Pig'n Whistle, a restaurant leaning heavily to sundaes, parfaits, and frappés, was the pot of gold at the end of shopping trips. While waiting to learn how my order of a chocolate soda with an orange float would shape up, I could gaze at the Art. All the walls were hung with paintings—Arthur Davies nymphs and woods, or children swinging through skies of what looked like authentically Maxfield Parrish blue.

Then, besides, there were the pigs. The lighting fixtures were fat, tiny pigs holding flutes. They blushed a tender pink when the lights were lit. Oh, Los Angeles, much could be forgiven for those pigs!

Sometimes, however, we went driving just for driving's sake. This seemed pointless to me. The adults exclaimed about the comfort and convenience of a motorcar in the same vapid way they talked about the vegetation. (*What, geraniums outside of pots?*) After we had driven to the top of Hollywood Mountain, one of the two highest peaks of our foothill range, I could see no reason to go up the other one.

The Gold and Silver Spider

To make my lot more endurable I was sometimes given company of what the grownups considered my own age—Agnes de Mille, for example, daughter of William and Anna, who was ten. *A dear little girl,* Mother wrote, *with whom Leaf* (my middle name is Greenleaf) *immediately was friends.*

To me the future choreographer of *Rodeo, Oklahoma!,* and *Fall River Legend* was no dear little girl. Being almost twice as old as I, she impressed me by her age alone, though I think she would have had some impact anyway. First, she had longer, redder hair than I. Second, she already shone with a little flame unconnected with the color of her hair. Third, I doubt if Agnes looked upon a plump, freckling five-year-old as a friend, but she was always interesting and, in that way, fun.

Climbing on foot was better than a drive. Mother and I made a lot of climbs, straight up from Bibi's house. In the early morning on the narrow trails we met lizards, rabbits, and a fox or two. We would slide most of the way home, scuffing our shoes, covered with dust and the scent of sage.

I took politer walks with Mrs. Borrodaile, a slender English lady Mother trusted to keep an eye on me. It was she who cheered me up about my evening meal at half-past five, before the grownups ate, by calling it my tea. After tea we hiked up to Krotona, a theosophical institute not far beyond the house. It was built like a pocket Taj Mahal. We would watch the lavender and yellow water-lilies close for the night in a reflecting pool. On our way home, clouds of midges danced against the sunset. Mrs. Borrodaile walked round the clouds but she didn't mind if I walked through. Lights went on across the street at the Myricks' and next door at the Saltmarshes' the pigeons cooed.

Like Mother, I was invited out. I spent several afternoons with Cecilia de Mille, aged eight, who sucked her thumb, and with Margaret, Agnes' sister, who was also eight, and with Caroline and Mary Smith who lived near them, up another hill. North of Hollywood Boulevard, you were almost always up a hill.

Hollywood When Silents Were Golden

Caroline and Mary had recently returned with their mother from a journey that was most unusual then—to Japan. They taught me to say *Ko go he-e-ka-ga-emi-ma-su-ka?* ("Is the queen coming?"), which could have been useful a year later when the King and Queen of Belgium paid a call on Hollywood. We children were sent out to strew flowers before the cavalcade, but I neglected my Japanese and we strewed in front of the wrong car.

The favorite game for all of us and our recruits was "London Bridge Is Falling Down." Margaret and Cecilia would be team captains and make tempting offers to woo us to their sides. Go with Margaret and you would have a silver castle full of golden furniture. Go with Cecilia and you won a catchall wish that everything you wished from then on would come true. This seemed the best value to me and I chose Cecilia. We didn't absolutely believe those promises, of course. And yet, having no television, no radio, and not many movies, we found entertainment in imagining. Imagination was still looked on as an ally, not an eccentricity.

Once in a while, if Bibi was engaged on "continuity" and Mother was involved with letters, which she wrote as regularly as she brushed her teeth, I would play alone. A small child whose parents Were Careful got pretty closely supervised, and outside the house I had to stay on the porch. I sat in a hammock, dangling my legs in ankle ties, long socks, and garters Grandma made. I stared into the giant dusty wig of vines. I would have liked to be with the Myrick children, opposite, but we didn't "know" them yet.

Perhaps it was because, sulky at being alone, I stared so very hard that I saw the gold and silver spider. It emerged from the macramé of ivy stems to the sound of distant drums: two typewriters—one upstairs and one down—and it sparkled as it scuttled over the woven mat. It was very small, the body no bigger than the head of the florist's pin with which Mother fastened a flower to her wolf-fur stole. But the body was all

silver and gold in a curious design I identified years afterwards as *yin* and *yang*.

I studied the gold and silver spider till it vanished in the ivy, then I went inside with my good news.

Nobody would credit it, of course. Nobody had ever seen or heard of such a spider. But as I always told the truth— telling the truth, not borrowing unless you asked, and never crying just because you had got hurt were a few of the commandments in our family—I was listened to, if quizzically.

I never saw the gold and silver spider again, never learned how many legs it had, never found its web. Its enchantment stayed in my catalogue of wonders of the world: peacock feathers, peacock colors in oil slicks and abalone shells, soap bubbles, rainbows, fireflies, tiger lilies, falling stars, mirage.

Soon we took a second trip on the mirage trail to the Valley, this time to watch Joan of Arc deliver Orleans. The walls of Orleans had been erected just across the draw from Domremy. Here, Mother explained, the loyal French of 1429— loyal to the *French* French king—were besieged by the troops loyal to the *English* French one, which meant the English king who also claimed the seat on the French throne. Joan of Arc, in favor of the former, meant to drive the English troops away and free the town.

The set was an imposing, costly one for a company so low in funds that not long before it had bought film by the strip from a competitor, instead of by the roll from a supply house. Four cameras stood in place to make the most of every angle of attack and of defense pouring down boiling oil (water heated by the July sun).

Joan arrived to begin the rescue on—of course—a big white horse. The horse must indeed have been picked for its color, not for its sunny character. Just as the Maid reined in beyond the English flank, the horse began to buck. Frantic shouts rose on all sides for Geraldine Farrar to get off. An investment in the thousands rode on every jolt and, besides, everybody liked the

star. A "double" would take on the riding, even if this did set limits to the scene.

Geraldine said no. She had subdued a pig and she would not be bullied by a horse. She headed into the fields and stayed in the saddle till the horse wearied of sunfishing and crowhopping. Then the hush above the armies, the battlements, and the weeds was broken with a general sigh that must have stirred the bells in San Fernando Mission ten miles away. Geraldine led a stirring charge and got off the horse to scale the walls.

Now it *really* seemed essential to bring in the double. "Boiling oil" splashed on star and extra alike. Water could be almost as dangerous as boiling oil to the operatic throat. But again the star said no. This was her role and her job and, like the Maid herself, she went over the crenellations into Orleans.

There was one last excitement to the day.

Rivalry in movie making was so fierce that scenes were actually pirated. A tremendous action sequence like this was a highly tempting prize. All day genuine cowboys had been circling the location to protect the prize. Now shouts rose from clumps of yucca and mesquite; shots rang out. Our cowboys had found camera poachers, rustling photographs! Mother presumed the shots were blanks. Still, in the Valley, the Old West was only yesterday. At Calabasas, just beyond the rise, "Baron" Leonis recently had ruled a little empire, through his marriage to a local Indian. Scant yards from his adobe grew a well-known hanging oak.

Driving home past Universal City that evening, we had a good look at Indians, in tents. These were not local. They had been imported to keep on hand for massacring cavalry outposts and assaulting wagon trains around the studio. Universal's new business manager, Jack Parsons, had instructions to lodge them in the Hollywood Hotel, but being a Westerner, he guessed how they might feel about four walls and veranda-rocking. So he let them make their own camp in the Valley instead, and, in appreciation, they took his little girl Virginia for

The Gold and Silver Spider

rides on ponies so untamed as to make Geraldine Farrar's white horse seem like a barnyard pet.

The last Lasky car drove away from Orleans, leaving cactus as the only weapon on the battlefield, and we arrived at Argyle Avenue with our quota of foxtails once again. Something seemed to stick in Mother's mind, as well. She remarked she might try her own hand at continuity, just for fun, of course. For my part I imagined Joan of Arc (or Geraldine) planting her pennant on our rooftop or the stairs. *Acting*, I thought, would be fun.

VI
Acting

Mother got a chance to exercise her inclination first—though I was right at her heels. *William de Mille has invited me to sit in on* The Heir to the Hoorah, she wrote her mother, and away she went on his location, for a closer look at how movies were being made.

While she was gone I had my chance to act.

Actually, acting was viewed with extremely mixed emotions at our house, even though a playwright couldn't well do without it. Mother frequently wished she could—faced with actors who fought or changed their lines, invented business of their own, had tantrums, caused delays. Yet she happily recalled performances by Forbes-Robertson, and Josephine Sherwood had added lustre to the Radcliffe presentation of *To Serve for Meat and Fee*. She had to be fond of some actors; my father, if he wanted to, could get along with *anybody*. Still, would you want your daughter to marry one?

Mother didn't say I was *not* to act and I can only assume that this came under the heading of Not Standing In My Way. The "other" children were doing it.

Agnes, Margaret, and Cecilia had already been on the screen. It was convenient, when a story called for children, to make use of ones you could control, and there wasn't much question in those days but that parents had control. In addition, Agnes, Margaret, and Cecilia were talented.

Acting

I had seen no performances by Agnes or Cecilia, but the first movie Mother took me to included Margaret in its cast. The movie was *The Heart of Nora Flynn,* directed by Uncle Cecil, starring Marie Doro. Mother and Bibi had agreed that generally movies were too stimulating for the young, but they thought I could retain my poise through this. They were right; the adult problems drifted over my head and the exciting part for me was the upsetting of a goldfish bowl.

As a warm-up to my acting career, I had already done one walk-on, when Mother and I went to watch William de Mille shoot some scenes at Tropico. Tropico, "the strawberry center," was the last stop in the Valley for the San Francisco trains before they reached Los Angeles. Most station scenes were made there. It was handy. The camera was simply set up to photograph the actors among passengers getting off. Nobody worried much about permission from the passengers—the problem was that the trains made very brief stops and sometimes nobody got off.

On the day of our visit, that's what happened, and we were rushed on the platform to "dress" the scene by boarding the train. We almost got swept off to the main depot. A few weeks later—it took very little time to finish and release a picture then—we glimpsed ourselves on a theatre screen, *just our backs fortunately,* Mother modestly wrote East. I, however, felt convinced that everyone must recognize us. Mother was swathed in her pongee duster. I was in mine, with a pongee hat as well, which looked like a mobcap bred to a soufflé. Had it been this striking performance which got me offered a part in *Witchcraft,* a story of Old Salem, starring Fannie Ward?

I knew something about Salem (you would have to, having lived in Boston as the child of Beulah Dix, whose most passionate crusade, next to pacifism, was destruction of the myth that Salem witches had been burned) and a little about Fannie Ward. She had acted on the stage so long that adults called her "ageless." Mother thought she was in her fifties but looked in

her twenties! Differences in any age over twelve were academic to me. What I'd heard about her husband, Jack Dean, fascinated me much more. We were told that he had had paraffin injections in his face, perhaps to stay as ageless as she, and that one morning when he fell asleep in an unfamiliar barber's chair, a barber applied hot towels, making the paraffin run into his chin. I didn't want to meet Fannie Ward half as much as I did Jack Dean.

However, it was Fannie I became acquainted with at Lasky Studio. I was already great friends with the director, Frank Reicher. Though he had no children of his own, or perhaps because he hadn't, he was a superb companion for a child. He took me swimming in the milder surf near Crystal Pier, where de Milles and Bucklands and Laskys picnicked and then sometimes dined at Nat Goodwin's restaurant on the pier. He and I sang German songs together. I was supposed to do well with "Ich Hatt' einen Kameraden" and "Morgenrot," two very tragic ballads capable of moving Mother to tears, which "Uncle" Frank and I delivered rollickingly.

So it was all right for me to report to work without Mother on the *Witchcraft* set. My eyes immediately fastened on the devils. There were two—men, I was aware—marvelously dressed up with horns and hoofs and furry legs. They *may* also have had bare chests. Naked male torsos were, however, not considered proper then and men's bathing suits were made with tops to them. Whether they were bare-chested or not, I accepted these amiable creatures (to whom I was politely introduced) in the spirit of satyrs rather than of imps. Bedtime reading at home leaned towards classical myths, not towards hell-fire. Whether satyrs or imps, they made Fannie and me, in our kerchiefs and long skirts, pretty drab.

We, too, set out on location, though only to the neighborhood of Domremy, which Mother had imagined might put me at ease. After all, it was already familiar even if it wasn't much like a New England glade.

Acting

The scene I was to play was short. Fannie and I would stroll down a path and then I would point out a devil sitting in a tree. Short or not, the scene was with a *star*. Alone with a star, as it turned out.

For there was no devil in the tree.

Fannie took my hand. We moved along the path. Uncle Frank gave a command for me to scream. At what? Both those devils, or satyrs, or whatever they were, had remained at the studio, perhaps currying their legs. How was I supposed to see one in a tree?

Uncle Frank explained. There had been no need to bring the devils to the Valley in the heat. (Foxtails in that fur?) When the picture was completed, by some laboratory hocus-pocus, my devil would be up there in the branches, right where I was pointing at him.

That was ridiculous, of course.

I had seen a gold and silver spider—yes. I had gone along with "London Bridge Is Falling Down." I had almost believed that Geraldine Farrar was Joan of Arc. *Someone*, at least, had been there in that costume running through Domremy and later up the walls of Orleans. Someone was beside me now in Puritan dress. No one was in the tree.

Uncle Frank was very nice. Fannie Ward, who, rumor said, could be difficult, was very nice. Just extend the play acting another step. Couldn't I pretend? Yes, of course I could! Dancing to any record in our house (except Chabrier's *España* which made me seasick), I pretended to be a glowworm, a blizzard, or an orphan. But for Uncle Frank and Fannie to assure me that an invisible man with hoofs would be visible, weeks from now, on film we were about to shoot, would have got them hung at Salem any time. Somebody was fooling them, but not me.

Patiently Uncle Frank and Fannie asked to me *try* to pretend. I did. We made our second journey down the path. As we neared the tree, Fannie squeezed my hand. I looked up and

stared. A live-oak tree. Branches. Leaves. I extended an arm and screamed.

Happily, no movie apparatus was extant as yet to record the scream, which I suspect was empty as the tree. Perhaps it would have been as well if the camera had not recorded my expression, either—the intent grimace of a child trying to oblige silly adults.

I never saw the scene on film, but that's the way it must have looked. I imagine I knew I wasn't a great acting success. (Would I rather be right than be a movie star?) Everyone continued being kind. We drove back to the studio, with my Puritan dress, my starched cap, and, I suppose, my box lunch a waste. *Witchcraft* went its further way, minus me. *Photoplay Magazine* gave it a review in 1917 as one of the fine American films which "lend tone and distinction to any theatre anywhere." I was not part of the tone; the small face left behind in that early cutting room was mine.

VII
Movies in the Mountains

Meanwhile Mother was in Big Bear Valley.

First of all, she had to learn how to spell the title of the William de Mille picture (which at the outset she wrote *Hurrah*) and, second, that location could be a lot more distant than the San Fernando Valley and would last for however long it took. Location still sounded marvelous to me, in spite of *Witchcraft*, for besides make-believe, it had the charm of picnicking and nature walks. I tried to imagine the fun Mother must be having.

While Mother was away, Mrs. Borrodaile spent extra hours with me and she told me that as a child she had been able to float from her bed (high upstairs in a house in northern England) down the stairs, still air-borne, and then drift unseen above the heads of family and guests. She heard their conversations and watched what they did. Truly, she assured me; she had floated in the flesh. Had any one glanced up, she would have been observed in her nightdress, horizontally suspended a few inches from the ceiling.

Until you knew Mrs. Borrodaile as well as I later did, she seemed a most unlikely person to indulge in fantasy or to eavesdrop, hovering in public in a nightdress, either. Her story caused the first rift in my firm faith that grownups never really had been children with a fierce impatience to their curiosity—impatience in adults mainly seemed to show in appetite.

Tucked in bed at seven, seven-thirty, and eight in those early years in Hollywood, I would close my eyes and try my best to flutter like a bit of flypaper or blotter just below the beams of Bibi's living room, sopping up the different laughs, the tinklings of glass, the puffs of smoke. Mother sometimes smoked, in order, she said, to look as busy and wise during silences at story conferences as men lighting up their cigarettes or knocking out their pipes.

My system never wholly worked, but I certainly drifted *somewhere,* for when I opened my eyes next, still in bed, there would be past-midnight darkness and faint past-midnight sounds. They meant that Bibi was alone downstairs, as she liked to be when all of us were stowed away, turning off the last lights, thinking, rearranging, hunting for her glasses, living a few minutes by herself in the center of her house.

More than anything, of course, I would have liked to float over the location at Big Bear.

Fortunately Mother wrote out the details and provided a picture nearly as clear as if I had peered down between the trees with my back against the blue.

We left Hollywood at 3:30, one of her letters began. That was a Saturday afternoon. The morning had been spent at the studio, with William de Mille shooting bar room scenes on an unroofed stage. *We motored to the Mission Inn. There we ran upon Constance de Mille and her party, who were returning from a long trip, and we foregathered joyously.* As Mother was accompanied by Anna de Mille and her children, there was quite a quorum of de Milles. (Bibi had had to stay behind to work.) The accidental meeting might suggest that all of Southern California was one big back porch. More accurately, places for foregathering were relatively few, in the minds of Mother's group, at least. The Mission Inn was a favorite. Though it had never been a mission, it had belfries, a chapel, cloisters, a crypt, and some less parochial assets, too. When it came my turn to visit there, I most preferred a life-

size wax-work reproduction of a Papal Court (even though a bat flew out of it) and the gift shop full of orange perfume and tiny bells.

At the Mission Inn, Mother got to bed at ten, before William de Mille and his actors checked in. Fifty miles on a narrow, humpy road could be quite a way and if you incurred a blowout, you might have to fit a new tire on your rim. *We tried for an early start,* Mother picked up her narrative next day, *but of course we didn't get off Sunday till half-past nine. First, a big company car, a Cadillac, with William, Miss King, our leading woman; Mrs. Neal, who plays her mother; the chauffeur; and three of our crew.*

Miss King was Anita King, a busy Lasky performer, and "Mrs. Neal" was Edythe Chapman (Mrs. James Neill), whose husband did character roles for the studio. Lasky, like the other companies, kept a group of stock players under contract, so familiar faces most often framed familiar stars. Except for a rare director like Griffith, and presently de Mille, pictures were sold on the basis of the public passion for the star. A title like *Carmen* didn't hurt and an author like Zane Grey had his fans, but it was widely held by picture makers then that most of the public couldn't read. You promoted your star—and to a small extent your stock company—and as much as possible, you held on to them.

Mother, unlike the public of the day, developed interest in the crew. She went on to specify, *Each director has an assistant director, a cameraman, an assistant cameraman, a property man, and a boy. The cameras are delicate and rather big to carry about.* She loved the country, too. *We spent most of the day in the desert, the real Mojave Desert, where more than one party perished in the old days. Now there is a good dirt road across it, but still you must be sure to carry water with you not only for yourself but for your machine.* She was amazed to find much of the desert hilly, though still all cactus, sage, and sand.

The William de Mille company was lucky that a cloudburst the day before had laid the dust, but this had created mud as well, in which the Cadillac—not the Overland in which Mother traveled, no doubt because the Overland was following —got stuck. It was dug out. This gave her time to note that there were clouds in the sky—a rare thing in these months in California. California clouds would, in fact, at no time of the year offer cameramen the variety and sweep of clouds over Europe or more eastern states.

The company had lunch at Victorville, a desert town which she called a sort of oasis on a stream. Then the real ascent began. She was being driven by what then was termed the back way to Bear Valley, behind the coast range, a much longer route than the one which went directly up from the city of San Bernardino, but less steep. Furthermore, the Millcreek Grade from San Bernardino was a one-way road. For four hours traffic could go up; for the next four it came down. If you missed your "control" you just waited, counting chipmunks or desert hares.

About three o'clock, Mother wrote, concerning the back way, *we began climbing into the hills, and clomb and clomb till we were at an altitude of about 6,000 feet. There we found beautiful mountain lakes and mountains clothed with pine, the most lovely and picturesque country you can imagine.*

It must have been a relief, yet also a slight sprain to Mother's convictions, to discover pines. One of her few quick criticisms of California had been that there were no trees. Since Hollywood had palms, eucalyptus, pepper, citrus, and acacia, and the foothills were full of live oak and scrub, she presumably meant trees in some other sense, like the groves in Waban or primeval forest.

Now in the California sierra, and not even in the High Sierra, she encountered heavy forest, but failed to mention this when she came home. Loyal to her pronouncement, I kept crunching through jacaranda pods, pepper beads, and acacia tassels, convinced I was trudging through a treeless waste.

Movies in the Mountains

The *Hoorah* cars had all collected at Big Bear Lake by nightfall, and the passengers piled out at Pine Knot Lodge. Mother called it *the gorgeous California idea of a hotel, a big log cabin, where meals are served, and then many little cabins in the pine grove surrounding it, where the guests stay.* She was tired and glad to get to bed in her cabin, after first removing "a dear little frog" which had planned to spend the night with her.

Mother was inclined to be quite calm about intruding wild life, even though leaving a tent in Vermont she had once walked into a bumblebee coming in, and acquired a poached eye. Not deft with inanimate objects, she was able to eject a daddy longlegs handily. The only creature she couldn't stand was a genuine spider, which may have been why she seemed distrait when I told her about mine, even though I had made plain that it was a smooth silver and gold, not—as she despised—the hairy kind.

On Monday morning everybody was away by nine o'clock, on location, about ten miles higher, at an abandoned gold mine. *Imagine sitting on the edge of a mountain, literally,* she described it, *and watching the shadows of clouds pass over the great Mojave Desert. The boys told us that we could see one hundred and fifty miles.*

Lunch was packed out from the hotel—sandwiches and pies, dispensed from the running board of the company car. Some friends of the de Milles turned up to watch the shooting—which prompted Mother to feel that even in the Sahara there would be onlookers if you made a film—and offered tea. They were rewarded with a mild excitement. Anita King was mounted on a burro. Her saddle slipped *in the middle of a take and she fell off with screams into the arms of the hero. That won't be publicly shown, but it will be preserved in the studio book of accidents, which few people see. Some of them are funny, but others are terrible. People get killed in this work oftener than the public knows.*

After this sinister aside, backed by no statistics, but quite

plausible—action was often improvised, unexpected, and hair-raising—Mother veered away to describe her sunburn, and concluded her letter to her mother, *It may not come off but at present it looks very much as if I should stay on here as a regular continuity writer for the Lasky Studio.* She had sometimes thought, she confessed, that it would be pleasant to be on a regular salary for a while—in this case, she specified with awe, a salary more than a Harvard professor got! While her husband's affairs were unsettled, it was perhaps wisest to grasp the opportunity.

She was back in Hollywood that Thursday, after an absence of five days, and I was glad to see her, with one reservation. While she was away I had been allowed to choose a present-a-day from among some parcels in the sunroom closet. The compensation almost had effaced the loss. One parcel contained a deck of cards with fifty-three photographs of movie stars (Charlie Chaplin was the Joker, of course) but, still better, in another I found a pencil a foot long.

VIII
Beulah Marie Dix: Playwright

My father's affairs certainly were unsettled.

They consisted chiefly in importing books: medical, magnificently illustrated, or occasionally racy. The racy ones were mainly for a little old lady in the Back Bay. She claimed she was maintaining a collection of her late father's, out of respect to his memory, but Father never felt too sure.

It became increasingly difficult to obtain books of any sort from countries engaged in war.

As a result, while most people moved to California for their health, to grow oranges, drill for oil, or hunt for gold, the reason we moved was World War I. Mother did find the movies interesting and an income attractive—she had had a dreary winter in 1916, publishing only a few short stories and proofreading her novel *Blithe McBride*, another of her books she didn't like. But the basic factor was the trouble which had begun overseas, somewhat earlier.

One morning at our breakfast table in the Boston suburb of Waban, when I was approximately three, Mother burst out, "Austria-Hungary has invaded Servia!" This she had, of course, discovered in the *Boston Transcript*. There was no other proper source, unless an even earlier-rising *Transcript* reader telephoned.

The history, geography, and even the humanity involved hardly touched me, but the tone struck home. Mother was in-

clined to pronounce even "Will you pass the butter?" with intense feeling. Small as she was, she must have been a grotto inside; her vocal resources were unlimited and when she lectured she could send her voice, unamplified, to the rafters of an auditorium. This led her later to scorn microphones even more than she did most mechanical things and stand aghast at actors and singers who preferred them. If she could project sound so well, without formal training, and encased in corsets, why couldn't professionals?

As to feeling, she released into her tone the emotions otherwise pent up by New England self-control. This disturbed my father. Much as he admired Mother and her writing—and he did, that was why he married her—he failed to understand why any human being wanted at a breakfast table to perform like the climax to Act Two.

Austria-Hungary's invasion offered mother an ideal occasion to present a dire piece of news dramatically. She was not hamming, though. She knew better than most women, most writers, and most readers of the period, that fighting would be hell even if it got labeled "a war to end wars" or "a just cause." In her mind, thanks to her research, were all those sordid facts it was not going to be patriotic to speak about for years (though she did)—namely, that looting, sadism, rape, massacre, and systematic starvation were not weapons merely of a depraved enemy; and that all of it was futile.

Over cereal, I knew only, of course, that Something Grownup Had Gone Wrong. I knew—and remembered—because of the tone, though it is just possible that the event stayed in my mind because the names were odd. We were eating, we were waited on, and she spoke of *Hungary* and *Servia*. Of such stuff is deathless recollection made. Later, we called that harried little country Serbia—before it turned into a part of Yugoslavia—but for me Servia kept its place in a mystic atlas compiled of such lands as lost Lyonesse and Jack's country up the beanstalk.

Beulah Marie Dix: Playwright

Europe itself was not quite all that strange to me, for I knew my father had been born there, and though by now he was a solid United States citizen, he and I spoke both English and German. A lot of young Germans, as well as young Americans, wandered through our house. They were part of a circle opened to Mother when she came to know the critic and writer Evelyn Sutherland, co-author of the play made from Booth Tarkington's *Monsieur Beaucaire*.

By that time, Mother had been well into her twenties, no longer quite a child wonder but still a youthful combination of bright cheeks, a buxom shirtwaist, and a tidy mind. Evelyn Sutherland, who was twenty years her senior, took her on as friend and collaborator. With her, Mother began writing plays professionally. Their *Rose O' Plymouth Town* and *Road to Yesterday* played both in and out of New York. Their *Breed of the Treshams* (written under a male pseudonym as better suited to so much leather and steel) was a staple of Sir John Martin Harvey's repertory in the English provinces.

Mother and Mrs. Sutherland traveled in the British Isles to work on and check on those and other plays. Mother found facing Highland cattle in a walk on the Isle of Skye as alarming as facing a first night. Mrs. Sutherland left her new best hat on a wardrobe in Dublin rather than miss a train. They traveled for their plays in the United States, too. Then when they came home to the Sutherland apartment in Boston, things were just as stimulating. Mrs. Sutherland was married to an eminent doctor, a wiry Scot marvelously energized by what we now call health food, of which he was a pioneer. (He, too, wrote—a formidable volume called *Malnutrition: The Medical Octopus*.) The Sutherlands kept open house for an enticing group of friends.

At least Mother found them so. The group centered upon Allan Rowe, the Sutherlands' adopted son of Mother's age, who was a doctor, too—his field was endocrinology. He brought home young men from Harvard, and from Göttingen,

where he had also done some studying. My father had studied at Munich, Oxford—and Göttingen. He even fought a duel there on Allan's behalf, since Allan, as a foreigner, could be insulted, but not qualify to claim "satisfaction" for it. I got Father to discuss dueling just once. I asked him why he didn't have a scar, which some people thought dashing, and he replied, "A good fighter doesn't get a scar."

When Father turned up in Boston, having left Germany for good to become a junior partner in a book firm, he of course entered the Rowe-Sutherland circle. Mother suddenly stopped acting like everybody's younger brother, seventeenth-century type.

She had never expected to get married. Statistically, for a bluestocking New England female, chances were poor. New England families she knew had mostly daughters. There had been few males to meet as she was growing up. Even at the Sutherlands', her blood ran cool. She liked her independence. She was satisfied with comradeship. But my father was so different from the other comrades! He was slight and strong, quiet and—to her—romantic (Allan mentioned that duel), personable, young, and she found it delightful that when he was angry, he looked scared. He was, in fact, a much better boy than she was, and she gave up forever being Tommy Drew.

Contented may not be the right word for Mother's marriage; *satisfied* might do. She did not regret it, and if there were some crashing silences those first few years—Father felt they got off to a rocky start when she dragged him, on their honeymoon, to look at every epitaph in every old graveyard on Nantucket—there was music, too. Mother wrote two novels of which Father was the model for the hero—*The Fighting Blade* (ancient) and *Mother's Son* (modern)—and some not-to-be-published love poems.

Real music rolled around our house in Waban. All the Sutherland group came, sometimes after beer at Jacob Wirth's or dinner on a visiting German naval vessel. The young en-

gineers and medical students, German or American, and a handful of young women, gifted and intelligent, sang together "Believe Me, if All Those Endearing Young Charms," "Juanita," "*Du, Du, Liegst Mir im Herzen,*" and "*Aennchen von Tharau,*" which Mother made a theme of *The Fighting Blade.*

Mother had fun.

She loved being hostess to the crowd surrounding Father in his velvet smoking jacket. She loved not knowing what young man, or what young men, might be in the extra beds on Sunday morning after a late Saturday night. She even loved the fact that after a Boston party, when she and my father wanted to stay over at the Copley-Plaza Hotel, due to a blizzard, they were refused a room because they had no luggage. That was quite different from being a woman alone on business in New York and finding there was only one hotel which would take in an unescorted female even with a ton of luggage!

Then there was Christmas. Christmas in her childhood hadn't been austere. Her beloved mother managed somehow, between cooking meals and starching petticoats, to make brand new clothes for every doll, even (perhaps especially) the boy dolls. But Christmas got still livelier in Waban, *gemütlich* right up to the attic where the German cook and maid had rooms. We all sang the carols and I got tossed high as the chandelier by the young men. I had trouble telling Uncle Allan Rowe from his cousin; one of them had a waxed moustache which prickled, but I couldn't always remember which. The house was filled with presents, wreaths, and an enormous tree, and I became a lifelong slave to marzipan.

Yes, Mother had *fun,* for the first time in her life. She could write as hard as ever, in her study, where she never was disturbed—I knew this rule so well, I was later told, that once, in a desire to communicate, I left a silent offering of animal crackers spread on the lintel of her door—and then she could step out to a husband, child, and home and, thanks to them, to new material for writing. Thanks to them, she was not a

mere part of the Sutherland circle, but a second center of it. This was a far richer world than she had ever expected, even after Radcliffe, and it broke apart just about the morning when she made that statement about Servia.

The German citizens got summoned home to arms. As a little boy, Father had been asked what he wanted to become when he grew up, and had answered, "Bismarck." But he had changed or he would not have left Germany. He had no desire to return. Still, it wasn't happy, watching the German friends leave, some of them reluctantly.

We never saw any of them after that. Some did not reach Germany—the British took them off American ships at sea and interned them. One died in prison camp on the Isle of Man. All that is left are photographs of smiling young men in college caps, photographs minus names.

The Americans of our circle we kept on knowing, though for the duration, some of them refused to speak, even Allan Rowe. Like the cause of the duel, the cause of this silence was never explained to me. Perhaps Uncle Allan had had second thoughts about the duel and decided it was barbaric, even in his own behalf? In the anti-German feeling of the time, that was possible. Your next-door neighbor of years might actually believe that the whole German army spent its time chopping off babies' hands or impaling them on helmet spikes. Men who offered any contradiction got sent to jail. Dachshunds were stoned. So it was not hard to lose a friend. Ten years later, we got Uncle Allan back again.

Mrs. Sutherland might have made a difference, kept the circle linked across the gaps, but she was dead.

One cold New England night when her husband was away, her dressing gown caught fire from the bathroom gas heater and the burns were fatal. Mother somewhat blamed herself. She often spent the night at the Sutherlands' when the Doctor was gone, and if she only had been there, perhaps she could have helped! But she didn't blame herself too much. Among

the cherished quotations by which she steered her life was a reference to "the impure passion of remorse." She considered it impure indeed. She scrubbed it out and named me for her friend.

Up to 1916, she did what she could about the war. At the risk of being labeled pro-German, she wrote two strenuously antiwar plays, *Moloch* and *Across the Border*. She even dared to claim that today's enemy can be tomorrow's ally. Holbrook Blinn starred on Broadway in both plays. They did not make money—not in the days of Nurse Edith Cavell and the *Lusitania*. When Mother got to Hollywood, she found Holbrook Blinn had already been there, recouping his losses with a few quick films. She was almost worn out by her writings and her feelings as we boarded that westbound train.

Now she was going to cash in our return ticket East.

In the fall of 1916 there was an infantile paralysis epidemic on the East Coast (no one then called it polio) which confirmed her decision not to hurry back. She went on the Lasky payroll in September, thinking she might stay as much as two years. My father prepared to join us, boxing up a few books, mostly for me—a history of France in volumes two feet tall and gorgeously illustrated German fairy tales. Next year we sold our Waban house.

I was a little sad about the house. I was fond of the attic, the stairs I frequently fell down, the glimmer of the coffee service (which got lost on the way West), and the big cushions in the library where we once ate sitting on the floor when our outdoor plans got spoiled by rain. In our yard, at the roots of a tall tree, there was quite delicious dirt. Best of all, in front of the vestibule which processed you in winter from the cold outside to the heat within, Father had planted a Surprise Garden for me. This meant he had sowed a plot of ground with an unlabeled packet of mixed seed. I had dashed out every morning of the spring to see what was coming up, but we took the train too soon.

This allows me now to imagine that perhaps a Venus Flycatcher has grown and thrives on Chestnut Street, Waban, oblivious to cold, trapping little children on their way to my old Sunday school. Or maybe there's a century plant, high as the spire of the church, flourishing half its way—after fifty years—to flowerhood.

IX
Beulah Marie Dix, Screenwriter—On the Lot

Bibi invited Mother and me to stay on at her house. Mother was immensely flattered. It must mean that I was as bearable as she'd hoped. I had a sound instinct not to cross Bibi, and I remember only once when she admonished me. She explained to me that like children, grownups—even Mother—had their rights.

Vulnerable about me, worried when it came to clothes (Father *would* say that Mother's hats looked like casseroles), Mother had a stern professional pride. *If I stay,* she wrote soon after Big Bear, *I work only with Wm. de Mille, who is a dramatist of equal standing with myself, so I lose no professional prestige.* William de Mille had made a solid stage success with *Strongheart*, a play which had no connection with the subsequent dog movie star of the same name, but was about an Indian.

More significant to me, he had also written *The Forest Ring* for children, an exciting story of the rescue of three bear cubs, and which had done its early bit (1914) in ecology. "We can understand," Antlers the Stag says to Arbutus the Fairy Queen in *The Forest Ring*, "That a man must kill to eat: and since he has such a useless skin of his own, that he should desire to keep out the cold with one of ours." What he and the other woodland creatures required was the Fairy Queen's help against a trapper who violated forest law by killing more than he could use.

As an infant vegetarian who stubbornly refused to eat anything I liked to pat (this excepted chicken), I could not have agreed more about Uncle William's prestige. In *The Forest Ring* he just went nowhere nearly far enough.

Few other published authors were at work in Hollywood in 1916. They might sell the movies a short story or a play—popular playwright Channing Pollock sold them twenty plays at one time—or they might drop in for a look. Somerset Maugham dropped in and it was Mother who was called on to develop an idea of his. But they didn't *live* here.

Now we did. Bibi and Mother turned what was to have been Mother's farewell party into a simple thank-you for hospitality received. It was not *too* simple. They gave it at the Town and Country Club on Mt. Washington, a scenic hill rising northward of Los Angeles Plaza and not far from the sites of the earliest studios, Lubin and Selig. The area had further charm for me because there was a zoo (with animals matriculated out of Selig adventure films) and an auto camp, the first one I had ever seen.

There were fourteen guests for lunch. They ate the fruit cocktail, jellied bouillon, Maryland chicken (preparation of which Mother described for the benefit of Her Sister Who Cooked, back there in New England), corn fritters, hot biscuits, honey. *The salad was of vegetables served in cucumber baskets. Then we had a chocolate ice cream with a rich ginger sauce, and cakes, and coffee. Also salted nuts, cigarettes, and a very good light punch of grape juice served throughout. At each place we had a dear little flower-holder with tiny pink rosebuds by way of souvenir.* Cecil Bruners, no doubt, which were new and captivating to us.

This was the end of being visitors. Now we had to remember for ourselves to take sweaters when we meant to stay out after dark and we learned to use the big red streetcar. I taught myself to ride standing up without touching anything at all, when it was full. We became fond of the little streetcar, the

Dinky, rather like a dinghy, which lurched along a spur line, taking us up Vine Street from the Boulevard to within a block of home. We began to shop on the Boulevard for other things than incense, tooth paste, and the eucalyptus lozenges I enjoyed so much even though Mother considered them medicine for colds.

Now Mother went to the studio every day.

For a short time she had a desk in Uncle William's office. Then she got an office of her own. She took quite a lot of trouble with it. After all, she spent more conscious hours there than in our bedroom looking out on orange trees. She brought the oranges into the office, draping windows and bookcases with cretonne in orange, black, and white. The windowseat was cushioned to match. In Los Angeles, she bought a wicker chaise, very tropical, and Japanese prints in a cold blue. On her flat desk, with its orange blotter, stood a black panther figurine with a surface pleasant to stroke, a Cornish cross, and a family of foxes in porcelain. Mother managed to identify with foxes.

I loved the office and was given freedom of it. Even though it was already difficult for outsiders to get into a studio, I could always pass through the wicket next to the front desk. Some people got stopped! Future producers, who as yet were office boys, waved them back. I went on, up a step or two, down a corridor that creaked. I liked the creaks because practice allowed orchestration—you just bore down on the proper boards. Mother's office was on the inside of the corridor, unlike that of Marion Fairfax Marshall, Lasky writer who had had a play on Broadway, too. Marion Fairfax's office looked out on the Vine Street pepper trees. Mother's looked out on the *lot*.

So I knew the lot in the morning—noisy, bright, and dusty in spots—when I walked down from Argyle Avenue with Mother. I knew it at lunch (we would go out, since there was no place for us to eat inside) when it grew quieter, the crews on their break. I knew it at night, not only coming to fetch

her home, but occasionally late, at a "running," as we called the showing of a film. Then it would be so quiet you could hear the cats.

There were quite a lot of cats, no doubt more than absolutely needed to keep sets and wardrobes de-moused. Now and then the studio money men—the ones who worried if they passed a writer's door and didn't see the writer actually pencil in hand at his desk—notified the pound to get the cats. Mother said that instantly all cats disappeared. After the pound had come and gone, they showed up again, having, she thought, been concealed by carpenters, painters, and gaffers practicing their own ecology.

When the studio, all wood and a block wide, caught on fire that fall, I'm not sure if it was Mother or the cats I was most worried about. Mrs. Borrodaile accompanied me to the blaze —within sight of it, that is. In the great tradition of "Austria-Hungary has invaded Servia!" I declaimed, "Catch me if I fall, catch me if I fall!" signifying I might swoon out of emotion.

"Certainly not," said Mrs. Borrodaile with a firmness that should have quenched the flames.

At all events, they were put out. (Hollywood had let itself be annexed to Los Angeles in 1910 mainly for the sake of a better water system, which presumably was useful here.) The cats seemed to be safe, and we found Mother had been shopping all the time. Mrs. Borrodaile and I retraced our steps past the corner orange grove and across the Boulevard, which I wasn't yet allowed to cross alone. Sometimes there was a policeman, an angular one who looked to me part wooden Indian and part semaphore. Sometimes there was not, in which case, as all left-hand turns were made then by going round the opposite car, not in front of it, there could be quite a traffic snarl—Mercers, Overlands, Franklins following each other's tail, a frozen carrousel. After we got through the traffic, there were three blocks of bungalows, which sometimes had a smaller bungalow in back for rent, modest duplexes, and larger bungalows which did *not* rent rooms. Then we were home.

Beulah Marie Dix, Screenwriter—On the Lot

One night Uncle Cecil came to dinner and gave me a special invitation to a running on the lot. This was an honor Mother couldn't decline, though she had her doubts about letting me see *Joan*. It was certain, she felt, to be a most overstimulating film.

The night of the running, the lot looked its most mysterious. The open stage—only one, at vast expense, had a glass roof—seemed to hold the shadows and vibrations of the scenes shot in their parlors or saloons. Water glinted in the tank where Uncle Cecil was shooting part of the sinking of the *Lusitania* for *The Little American*.

Mother and Bibi had been onlookers at the other part, off San Pedro. They had driven to the port, by invitation, only to find that *The Little American* company was already out at sea. They had made up their minds just to buy some shells and enjoy the view when Mary Pickford's mother arrived. Mary Pickford was the picture's star, and her mother had no intention of being kept from her side, so she chartered a launch and invited the two other stranded guests along.

We pursued the elusive C.B. and found him with his forty-odd company and assistants, with two large trucks and five cameras perched on a big flat, with two launches beside him, somewhere off the coast of California. Mary Pickford, too. *Great excitement on the flat as they beheld the two heroic mothers approaching.*

The disembarkation, in Mother's view, was spectacular. The ladies had to make a long leap from their bobbing launch, but four stalwart young property men boosted and pulled, and they landed safely. *We stayed there till eight o'clock and saw several very interesting and perilous shots made. I admired the courage of the extra girls who went over into the water.* I did, too, as Mother reviewed all this enroute to the projection room. Even near the shore, the semitropical Pacific wasn't warm. I was already pretty stimulated by the time I sat down in my hard folding seat.

Joan the Woman was a fine picture and a long one. When

the scene unwound which Mother felt I really mustn't see (Joan was being interrogated), she had to wake me up to tell me not to look. Then she decided I had better look, after all, for Geraldine Farrar's expression—as Joan's hands were plunged in boiling water—was sublime. After that, nightmare prone herself, she waited apprehensively for a reaction in my dreams.

There was no reaction at all, except that the close-up of Farrar remains more vivid for me than the whole of Carl Dreyer's much later, brilliant *Passion of Joan of Arc*, which was almost entirely close-ups.

Soon after this, Mother trotted me up Krotona Hill without a qualm to see *The Light of Asia* performed in the evening, out of doors. What could be more harmless than a dramatization of the life of Buddha?

The black foothills leaned over the white dazzle of the stage. A coyote barked (possibly a dog) and an owl hooted (possibly an auto horn) as the sheltered young Prince Siddhartha left his palace for the first time and encountered a pauper, a leper, and a corpse. I had some idea about a corpse (Halloween and all that) and Mother very kindly enlightened me about begging and leprosy.

Caught up in the spell of the play—Walter Hampden, with a solid reputation in dramatic classics, was the star—Mother didn't seem aware how close I kept beside her on our hike home. But she grew aware, all right, when she had to leave a night light burning for me for the next five years. Not Saint Joan's inquisitors, but the benign Buddha had evoked images for me which I had no wish to bump against alone in the dark.

X
Hollywood Forty-six

Father got off the train at the Green Hotel in a Santa Ana, the local gale which gave us credentials for an exclusive group of wind-plagued areas: north Africa with its sirocco, southern France with the mistral, Zurich and Munich with the foehn.

We gritted our way through the sandstorm back to Bibi's house, where he, too, settled in. This two-family arrangement worked extremely well. Mother and Bibi kept each other company while he was on field trips for his new job in the oil industry; when he was at home, he and Bibi got up games of bridge. Household costs were shared. Mother was an advisor; Bibi was the manager.

Mother was enchanted. She held to a solemn belief that a woman shouldn't try to mix housekeeping and career. "You cannot do two things at once," she would repeat. Fortunately Bibi could. In spite of her scenarios, she handled menus and servitors with careless ease. We had quite a turnover in servitors for a while—they moved through the house so fast they hardly had time to learn about the sliding door.

Bibi remained undismayed. She had once run a girls' boarding school near New York, with bewitching Evelyn Nesbitt among the girls, and the complications of that sixteen-year-old beauty's courtship by Stanford White, Harry Thaw, and John Barrymore added to more usual stresses of budget and curriculum.

Some of the stresses at Argyle Avenue relaxed when Joe Kamemura moved into the basement and later, with a picture-bride to help, seemed enthusiastic about gardening, cleaning, cooking (even puff pastry)—and us.

Actually, Bibi stopped doing scenarios, but at once launched into other projects. She redecorated. Mr. Espino, an artist of unbounded versatility, created for her a six-foot standing lamp, the base in grey, twined with life-size red poinsettias (gesso) that could give you a nasty poke. He also put artificial shadows on the ceiling so that in the living room it was always half-past five of a sunny afternoon; and he painted hunters stalking tigers round the sunroom.

Bibi thought of building a bungalow court with Mr. Espino and it seems a shame the plans fell through. Hollywood was noted then for eateries shaped like hot dogs and cottages with imitation thatch. It already had a bungalow court like a Normandy village and another like Topkapi. Perhaps a Zulu *kraal* for de Mille–Espino?

In her building mood, Bibi offered me a game room in our orchard. Among the local sights to which we had been hurrying Father was the Arrowhead Springs Hotel, an elderly structure slumped on rising ground just back of San Bernardino. There the adults took mud baths, drank from sulphur springs, and strolled. I rode a mule, and fell in love with a non-profit pinball machine. Bibi said I could have a machine like that, and other interesting apparatus, in the game room. All that was asked of me was to make a sketch.

That should have been easy. I sketched all the time and had sketched our way out on the train. After we saw our first live Indians at Albuquerque, I drew nothing except Indians for a long time. Mine all wore spectacles because the blanketed brave from whom we bought a toy on the platform was wearing them. Finally, to everyone's relief, I picked another subject—females. But my females all had figures like boards, and Mother inquired why. What a stupid question. I was flat chested, wasn't I?

Hollywood Four Six

Perhaps the question shook my self-confidence. I kept thinking I might botch the game room, forget doors or windows—even not care for the pinball machine after all. So I never finished the sketch, and the game room never was built, any more than the de Mille–Espino bungalow court. Where the game room was concerned, it turned out just as well. Several peach trees would have had to be cut down, and a few years later we had a German shepherd dog so fond of peaches that when he could not find windfall on the grass, he sprang into the air and snatched the peaches off the tree.

Bibi shrugged, moved the three of us upstairs to a converted porch, and added a glassed porch downstairs. Her ninety-year-old mother, Mrs. Samuel, came West to stay, with Emma Opitz, who was officially her companion, unofficially a saint. Mrs. Samuel was slim, straight-backed, black-eyed, with a floss of silver hair. She lived more in a private world than in her suite, except for a moment every night when Father called on her, glass in hand. "There is that nice young man," she would exclaim, her eyes twinkling, "who brings me something to drink!" Then she would sip her small martini with the elegance of a Sargent portrait brought to life.

Father's arrival had a slightly more than average interest for Mother's group. *I have already encountered two Flebbe legends,* she wrote. One, circulated at the studio, was that he had just landed from Germany, *presumably with dispatches, on the U-53.* Though the United States was not at war, a German submarine had achieved quite a feat in running the British blockade to our East Coast. The other story was that Father was an Englishman. It was a broad choice, made more piquant by Bibi's calling him "Captain"—mostly, Mother thought, to tantalize Veda Buckland, who was wildly curious.

Father accepted the title—you did not lightly refuse Bibi's gifts, as I knew, still hangdog over the game room—but the nearest he ever got to captaincy was heading up a bowling team. Generally there was much less anti-German feeling in

Hollywood When Silents Were Golden

California than in the East, though we did know a family that kept their car stocked with supplies in case of need to flee into the desert from an enemy. This should have made them quite blasé when it came to West Coast air raid scares in World War II.

Father the Captain did set us on a slightly different course —not so many lunches and teas and views, more picnics and participating sports. We went picnicking in rocky San Gabriel Canyon with the de Milles and left quickly when our first earthquake twitched the rocks. We went to the Cawston Ostrich Farm, where I had my picture taken while he held me on an ostrich, and the alligator farm (no picture), and then there was the beach.

With Father, the beach was not an outing, it was a seven-hour day. If you got there Sunday morning by eleven, you avoided the "heavy" traffic, usually missed the fog, and could finish eating, swimming, and playing ball—Father liked all games, not merely bridge—with daylight and determination left for the amusement pier.

This program could be adapted to fit me into Sunday school, but not to extend to church. However, for the moment, Mother was antichurch. She had taken me to the brown church beside the Vine Street orange grove when we first arrived, sitting warily next to a door. The thing she greatly feared had come to pass: the minister spoke with a dreadful Western twang and even patronized the Lord! So when a nice-looking gentleman beckoned from outside, she was relieved. We slipped quietly away.

The gentleman was Jimmy Young, a Lasky director and the husband of dark-eyed, intense actress Clara Kimball Young, who in 1914, had ranked ahead of Mary Pickford in a film star popularity poll. He and Mother had already met and he felt a mission to buy me ice cream. His heart had bled when he noticed a small child squirming on a slippery bench on a hot day while some adult droned. From then on my favorite director

was, of course, Jimmy Young. Mother had second thoughts. Mr. Young was in the process of directing a picture Bibi wrote and of making changes in it, too. He offended Mother by asking questions, trying to learn Bibi's opinion of him. Some weeks later when she saw his movie *The Lash*, Mother forgave him. It contained, she thought, some of the loveliest sea pictures ever shot. *He is a painter with the camera.* What else should she have expected from a being sensitive enough to diagnose a Sunday morning need for ice cream?

We had lots of ice cream at the beach, in cones which dripped faster than they could be licked in a strong noon sun. We sat on blankets under our umbrellas waiting out the hour after food till it was safe to swim, but sometimes prolonging it with just one more hard-boiled egg stuffed whole (though peeled) into our mouths.

Mother considered people dressed more sensibly for swimming, out here in the West. Plain wool suits reached only to the knees, fewer bathers had on stockings and shoes. Some of our friends did remain covered up—Anna, Agnes, and Margaret de Mille, for instance, whose skins were exquisitely fair. As for me, no appearance could compare, when we reached the water's edge, with Madam Glyn's.

Elinor Glyn was the author of the most daring fiction of the day. (Sheer pornography, some people called *Three Weeks*.) She did not set foot in the sea carelessly. When I saw her, she wore a black, ruffly, short gown—taffeta, I believe—black stockings, shoes, and gloves, and a black bonnet on her brightly red-gold hair. Her eyes were vivid green and her whole face had a charmingly enameled look. She approached the breakers as her heroines approached seduction on a tiger skin. What wave would have dared to tumble her?

Even in Southern California, the beach season reached a close, though there were some wonderful hot October, November, and December days. The adults turned to greater night life, not too formally. A tradition was already born that Holly-

wood men did not dress for dinner. This was because they stayed to work on the set until the last light, so they were late enough for any social occasion, without going home to change.

But the women could dress, so Mother had a dress made. It was designed by a lady who came near to living at our house for several days, much as if we were an isolated plantation of the Old South. Some of the sewing was done by Mrs. Borrodaile, no mean hand at design herself, and by Emma, who had all domestic arts. Even for a new dress, some old fabric was used. (Having a professor's salary did not mean you should lose your head!) The point of departure was a beaded stole Mother had worn at her wedding reception.

Under the stole went layers of stuff—pale green net with silver beading, a white slip with a flounce of silver lace, a pink slip cut low at the neck but hastily filled in with tulle. There was also a pale pink sash with a deep pink rose, *the one strong note of color*, Mother wrote and added—nervously?—*it is really much more stunning than it sounds. Broock nearly fell dead when he saw it.*

Broock was a nickname for my father derived from *The Fighting Blade*. I'm not sure if he nearly fell dead, but he never said a word about the dress. He undoubtedly would have preferred it to the uniform Mother chose for the studio—a corduroy skirt, a blouse with an orange tie, a leather jacket, and boots. He liked lavish, fluffy things, giving gifts, and paying compliments. Mother was embarrassed by compliments and never could conceal the fact that she had little use for perfume, jewelry, or hand-embroidered lingerie—his kind of gift.

The dress was christened on election night. Marion Fairfax and her husband Tully Marshall, who played "Fagin" to Marie Doro's starving "Oliver," gave a dinner party. Mother, Father, Bibi, Marie Doro and Elliott Dexter, Fannie Ward and Jack Dean, and Charlie Chaplin were among the guests. Charlie Chaplin was a new neighbor of the Cecil de Milles, and my family had met him previously at Marie Doro's. *Rather a*

bounder, Mother had felt, and didn't think his newest film, shown at the party, was at all funny—there was too much "How wistful I am" about Chaplin.

She liked him better when, after the Marshall dinner, the guests went to a little theatre. *We saw a very poor and nasty play from the Russian,* Nyu, *very badly given by amateur actors,* Mother set down. *Wm. de Mille said it was "a Maeterlinckian miscarriage."* Jack Dean sat beside her and said, "Oh God!" at intervals. Charlie Chaplin was right behind *making ribald remarks in a low, soft voice.*

The group moved on for supper and to hear the election returns over a private wire. California was one of fifteen states where women already had the vote. Mother hadn't yet been able to register, but she was immensely interested. If Woodrow Wilson were made president again, it would be, she thought, because of the women's vote. The women didn't want their country in a war and he had promised not to get into the war. So when the result proved in his favor, late next day—the count was close—she assumed we would have peace. Mother was a doubtful prophetess. She also believed that of the two rival telephone systems then in use in Hollywood (you had to subscribe to both or be out of touch with half of your friends), the *non*-automatic one would be the one to last. Who would rather dial a string of numbers than ask a friendly operator for our simple Hollywood four six?

The second time she wore her new dress was for Thanksgiving. This was a Progressive Dinner.

There had been a Progressive Dinner at the William de Milles', where the guests sat at tables for four, and after every course, the men moved to another table. *Our* Progressive Dinner was yet more active. Every different course was at a different house. We served cocktails at Argyle Avenue. Oyster soup was at the Tully Marshalls', turkey at Uncle Cecil's—with some extra trimmings by Bibi—salad at the Bucklands', pumpkin pie, ice cream, coffee, and liqueurs at the William de Milles'.

We all walked the two blocks from the Bucklands' to the William de Milles' in such a drowsy silence of late afternoon that you could hear a pepper berry drop and Carrie Jacobs Bond, at the piano in her house up the hill, improvising a new "Perfect Day."

For the other courses, we had needed cars, and the Progressive Dinner languished soon after when, thanks to traffic, half a day would be required just to reach the homes of half-a-dozen friends.

The year ended with Mother completing her first continuity —based on someone else's work, as it happened, not her "original." It was *Prison Without Walls* and would star Wallie Reid. She wrote East enthusiastically, *this is theatrical work, with all its joys and drawbacks.* How much the drawbacks were outweighed by joys. Lots of it was working out-of-doors!

On Christmas Eve I was bitten by a baby gopher, while play acting with the Myrick children that it was a baby squirrel, which no doubt would have bitten me with equal zest. No one took much notice. All the Lasky employees had brought home presents from the studio. Mother's was a twenty-five-dollar gold piece. This was like a more comfortable, less illiterate, Days of '49! We had had our first six months of Hollywood.

XI
School Sets In

Without the United States, the Allies would run out of troops, Mother pursued her hopeful train of thought, and there would be peace all round.

A contrary omen appeared that January, just about coincident with my birthday (Bibi and I had the same birthday, also an omen surely, but a pleasant one), when Mrs. Borrodaile's son Osmond got his orders to ship out.

Mrs. Borrodaile had migrated with her parents to the neighborhood of Calgary as a young girl and married a Mountie in charge of a troop sent to protect her family's ranch during Indian trouble. Now Osmond was about to face trouble, too.

He was, of course, Canadian. He and his mother had moved to Southern California with a brother recuperating from a rodeo injury. There seemed no end to the adventurousness of the Borrodailes! Osmond was now in basic training near Vancouver—he was eighteen, so middle aged to me, so young to everybody else. Mrs. Borrodaile got on a ship for Vancouver. Mother wept for her and ached a little—less nobly—for herself. She was busy with two scripts; Father left for his desk at the Ventura Refining Company at eight; Emma took care of six canaries and Mrs. Samuel.

Mother would never find another Mrs. Borrodaile to look after me, but she need not have worried about Osmond. He not only outlasted World War I to become Alexander Korda's

brilliant cameraman on *Henry the Eighth, Elephant Boy,* and *Sanders of the River* (and to make an Academy Award documentary on the home life of the gannet), but he also was a combat cameraman in World War II, clambered up cliffs in Ethiopia with Emperor Haile Selassie, survived a bomb in Cairo and torpedoing in the Atlantic.

Meanwhile, now that I was unsupervised, for my survival (broken glass, abandoned iceboxes, heedless motorcars, and Children With Bad Habits were what Mother had in mind), I had better go to school.

I was glad to go. Everybody who was anybody went to school by now: Naomi Myrick, Caroline, Cecilia, Margaret, Agnes, Midge next door, who could kick above her head, and the boy down the street who hooted at me "Red!" or "Brick!" The question was, what school?

There was a public school, Cheremoya, half-a-dozen blocks away. Cherimoya (I don't know how the spelling became modified) was a fruit, I found out, whereas Micheltorena, a school we passed part way into Los Angeles, referred to a family. We were always setting pronunciation traps for Easterners—Ojai, La Jolla, La Cienega, San Xavier—with our Indian or Spanish names.

By herself, Mother might have plumped for Cheremoya. The public school system in New England had done well for her. But my father's background surfaced here. A boy in Europe, and a girl especially, had to attend a private school. Otherwise you couldn't grow up to belong to the officer class or, presumably, marry into it. Father never longed to be an officer—he was late for his military-service interview, ran up the stairs, and got rejected for a racing heart—but he wanted the choice and he wanted it for me. Things might be somewhat different in the United States—but not *that* different.

I visited Cheremoya once. Virginia Parsons, who had done all that galloping around with Universal City Indians, was going there. But the decision reached was that I wouldn't fit.

School Sets In

There were several well-established, sound, local private schools for girls. The problem was that quite a few would not admit children from movie families. This was not a discrimination against movie *children;* several clubs barred their doors for years to movie adults. Whether we were deemed immoral, uneducable, insolvent, or all three, we were felt by Los Angeles business and society not to belong.

Scratch three more schools.

What about the funny little school at the western end of Hollywood, on La Brea Avenue?

Agnes, Margaret, Cecilia, and Cecilia's young half-aunt Nancy Adams (such a wonderful expression, half-aunt, almost mythological) were already enrolled. Mother went to look and came away content. There was a feeling in her circle then that formal education should be given late and sparsely to the young. She didn't think that at the Hollywood School for Girls I would get taught *too much* or have my spirit broken. It should be hard to feel even psychologically fenced in when half the classes were held outdoors!

The Hollywood School for Girls had been established on Hollywood Boulevard in 1911—suitably enough, the year I was born—with the object of encouraging sensible manners (never cross your legs, unhealthy as well as impolite), good health, and intelligence. A few years later it was transferred to La Brea Avenue, as businesses on the Boulevard grew, and sold by Miss Sophie Hogan to Miss Louise Knappen. Miss Louise Knappen maintained the elevated standards with, I felt, one signal lapse. She got *married,* in 1917. I could hardly have been more shocked if the marble statue from Robinson's department store had walked across the lawn in bridal dress.

In time, we got used to Miss Knappen as Mrs. Woollett. Her husband was the innovative architect William Lee Woollett, who had already much enriched my own experience through his creation of the glittering, elaborate Million Dollar Theatre in Los Angeles, where we saw many favorite films, among them

a short subject in which a judge (Cecil Holland) demonstrated the art of applying make-up. Two years later Lon Chaney was to play the first of the grotesque roles ("The Frog" in *The Miracle Man*) which would give him lasting fame in *The Phantom of the Opera* and *The Hunchback of Notre Dame*. I was well prepared for that by having watched the judge change to the suave, the saintly, and the sinister on the Million Dollar screen before my eyes.

The Hollywood School for Girls was without glitter. Mr. Woollett taught a course on the History of Art, but the school never looked as if it had an architect. La Brea Avenue was a residential street, barely scarred with duplexes, and the school's Main House was a residence. It was a respectable two stories, far from stately, able to accommodate some half-a-dozen boarders, provide ten or twenty hot lunches, and hold half the student body (which from kindergarten through high school numbered not more than a hundred girls) at a musicale.

Mrs. Woollett kept her office in the glassed entry of the residence. Here, at crises in exams or student government, you had your confrontation. Though mothers who knew her well found her gentle and compassionate, she looked rather like a Roman senator and made me ill-at-ease. I avoided the office and adored the school.

If you arrived by car, you were dropped under acacia trees at the Main Gate. There was, in fact, no other gate, though even at six you could easily get over the stone wall along the sidewalk anywhere—it was sitting-down high. There was no real gate, for that matter, just a space in the wall for a carriage drive which led straight back past the Main House. This was our access to the classrooms at the rear, and a forum and playground as well. No one drove on it, of course.

As you walked up, leaving the acacias behind, the jacaranda on the lawn, and the rose garden by the house, you would cover a hundred yards before you thought you were inside a school. Then you came upon the sculpture studio, the music

School Sets In

department, the lower classes buildings, the chemistry lab, the study areas, the history and language divisions, the newspaper ready-room, the athletic field, and the high school auditorium.

The auditorium, wood, looked like the first cousin to a barn. (Every building in the school was wood, though some suggested papier mâché.) The ceiling must have been twenty feet high and one whole side was made of doors. The newspaper room was an adjoining closet. The history and language divisions each had a twelve-by-twelve bungalow. The chemistry lab was ten-by-twelve. The lower classes buildings were a trifle larger (which in winter made them colder) and all but enclosed the "athletic field" (asphalt), affording unwilling backboards for baseball and basketball. The sculpture studio was an arbor with a concrete floor, which made the modeling clay nice and damp. The music department was a piano in a hut.

In addition, there were Facilities, (rather limited—if you *insisted* on a shower after basketball, you could take one in the Main House), a lean-to where the janitor attended to repairs—and lived, I suspect—and our Woodcraft lodge, a shanty behind the auditorium among the castor beans. Even before we were old enough for Woodcraft, we were warned not to eat the beans.

What made up for the casualness, the occasional discomfort, even shabbiness, was that much of the teaching did go on out-of-doors, and much of the studying as well. Green benches ringed a huge pepper tree, which also had a tree-house available for those minus vertigo, and benches and tables stood beneath a giant pine. The teachers ranged from young and charming to grey-haired and challenging.

Then there were the girls. When I first trudged up the drive in my brown crepe dress with bloomers to match (so that if I climbed the jacaranda or some other happy hazard, I would not reveal a vulgar flash of white) there were a lot of interesting girls wriggling, drifting, or running around H.S.G. They were not all "movie girls." Some came from the neighborhood:

Katharin (without an *e*), who happened to live next door to Chaplin Studio, and Katharine (with an *e*), whose father, a dentist, had some motion-picture patients.

Others were from even less affiliated worlds. We had a Fowler (books), a Toberman (real estate), a Bireley (soft drinks), and presently a Felix (cars). I remember Muriel Fowler because she didn't stay long, Catherine Toberman because she did, Ruth Bireley because she smiled, and Alice Felix for her Spanish eyes.

Then there were the girls whose names you cannot forget in themselves—Mary Hogg and Josephine Pigg, who were in school at the same time. Mary was small and Josephine was tall, but both must have had sublime natures to support unending witticisms.

Still, the motion-picture girls gave a distinctive twist to the student body. Besides the de Milles, there was Ruth Lasky, Jesse Lasky's niece, whose mother had divorced producer Samuel Goldwyn and resumed her maiden name. There was a daughter of Reginald Denny, a rising star of comedy-romance, and a daughter of Francis X. Bushman, an established star as far back as 1912.

Joan Burroughs, whose father had invented *Tarzan*, perhaps was not exactly "movie," but belonged among the children of celebrities, too. She was fair, and in her riding clothes—at H.S.G. we had riding, swimming, dancing, fencing, theatre parties, and made batiks and lamp shades, to offset the mental strain—she appeared to me such an aristocrat that a few years later I could only think of her when I sneaked into the hammock in our back yard to read about Lady Diana Mayo who looked like "a damn pretty boy and a damn haughty one" in *The Sheik*. Mother had banned *The Sheik* for me, not because she thought it was corrupt, but because she thought it trash.

When I entered H.S.G., however, the most dynamic girl of all, then in high school but making waves down to the bottom class, was Irene Mayer, whose father, Louis B. Mayer, would

School Sets In

be almost as much a symbol of the biggest studio with its biggest stars as the Metro-Goldwyn-Mayer lion itself.

Irene's eyes sparkled and her hair shone, both very black. She had a handsome face, vast vitality and wit, and she must have had warmth, for she was not frightening. Even the smallest of us went to a benefit in the auditorium where she was impresario and auctioneer.

I was afraid to bid my twenty cents (get noticed by all forty amateur adults in the upper school?), but offered silent admiration to such poise, and loud laughter at her spiel. She whipped up quite a whirl of bidding, to earn several dollars for a worthy cause, probably perpetuation of the school's monthly paper, *Pine Points*. Therefore it offended me deeply when *Pine Points*, publishing a column of students' names linked with thumbnail character impressions, coupled "tarantella" with "Irene." I had loved that gold and silver spider but I didn't believe Irene Mayer seemed like a tarantula, even a good-looking one.

XII
Beulah Marie Dix—Original Story and Continuity

Back with the black, white, and orange cretonne, Mother got good marks more rapidly than I.

Having begun her career with useful comments on *The Heir to the Hoorah*, she next tackled some revisions *to help William out*, whisked off two continuities, and was watching the shooting of her original story *The Cost of Hatred*. (She was also working on another adaptation, *The Girl at Home*.) The directors call "Ashes of Hatred" (her original's first title) *as nearly perfect as a script can be. God keep us from vanity!* she wrote.

She jotted down that by May 13, 1917, she had written eight "shootable scripts" since January first, quite an output even though scripts were shorter then and titles, whether explanatory (*Came the Dawn*) or "spoken" (*Kiss Me, My Fool*), generally were completed after shooting. She liked to work in frantic spurts, which could not have made her popular with colleagues who took twice the time. She got the smiles of the money men, though, till they discovered that if she compressed eight hours' worth of concentration into four, she not only didn't want to sit at her desk, pencil in hand, she would go home!

As to her colleagues, she never much cared for writers as a group. She found many of the men finickily intellectual and many of the women fools, if often clever fools, what later would

be termed phonies—women who coquetted and connived and plagiarized to success. She didn't care about their morals in the least; it was their ethics which offended her. They traded on their relationships with men (all right in history, she felt, but not in art!) or they even *advertised*. She would no more have advertised herself as a writer than she would have advertised as teacher, wife, or mother. This *may* have contributed to her remaining, through more than twenty active years in the motion picture industry, rather little known.

A few writers she liked very much. One was Frances Marion, a beautiful ex-newswoman. Mother claimed that Frances could write a serious and poignant script for Mary Pickford with one hand and a roaring Oater for her husband, Western star Fred Thompson, with the other. Like Jack Dean with his paraffin, such physical peculiarity intrigued me so that when Frances Marion came to tea, I peeked through the bannisters to see how ambidextrous she really was. Alas, she handled a cup like anybody else.

Mother also liked Eve Unsell, who had furnished her and Evelyn Sutherland with the basic material for their play *Stigmata*, a horrendous tale about a fallen woman (More To Be Pitied Than Censured—she had been seduced and deserted very young), who reformed, took the veil, had her past exposed, and was being walled up alive when, as a reward for her sufferings, nail marks appeared on her palms.

Phyllis Neilson-Terry, the striking-looking English actress who tried out the play in Wolverhampton, wrote Mother, "I think we have got a really big success," though she did add a little wistfully that people seemed amazingly ignorant: very few, except Catholics, knew what Stigmata meant, "so we shall have to do a little explaining to the Press." The explaining evidently wasn't quite enough to bring *Stigmata* into London or over to the United States, but Eve Unsell journeyed West to be a screenwriter and we saw a lot of her.

Of all the women scenarists, we saw most of Jeanie Mac-

pherson, who was credited with the majority of Uncle Cecil's scripts. Mother never really thought of her as a *writer*, but as an exceptional collaborator for an exceptional man. Uncle Cecil, with his past experience in writing and acting and his unsurpassed showmanship, knew not only what he required in every story he directed, but in every scene. Jeanie had a genius (for some reason everybody called her "Janie," so there is no alliteration) for putting this on paper.

We were with Jeanie quite a lot, at the studio and at the de Milles'. She was most remarkable at openings (as we termed premieres), for, though somewhat angular in feature, she wore the frilliest of clothes. When occasion warranted, she was inclined to picture hats. Better suited to her looks was her hobby of collecting jade.

Mother respected Jeanie, except in one area. Jeanie couldn't punctuate. Bertram Millhauser, with whom Mother was teamed in writing some de Mille pictures, claimed that after the titles for a picture had been worked out, Jeanie stood across the room and threw periods and commas at them as if at dart boards. It reminded Mother of that hero of her Massachusetts youth "Lord" Timothy Dexter, who dotted half-draped statuary round his Newburyport lawn, sold warming pans to the West Indies (making a fortune—the pans were utilized in sugar refining), and crowned his vagaries by publishing a book devoid of punctuation till the end, where he supplied some pages of it to be used at will.

Mother met other women, besides writers, on the lot. She sat in a dark and airless cutting room with Anne Bauchens, who would rise to eminence as Uncle Cecil's chief film editor, and with Dorothy Arzner, who would leave cutting to direct. She even found a staunch friend in a reader, much as she deplored the existence of readers as a whole. Looking on them as Fallen Writers, she felt sorry that they were so miserably paid; on the other hand, she couldn't comprehend the need for what they did. How could any human being delegate his reading to somebody

else! The logistics involved in sifting through the mass of story submissions studios received even then impressed her no more than did the mechanics of the dial telephone.

With some help from women *and* men, Mother also worked on set and costume breakdowns for her films and on the choice of cast. She found it all exhilarating. It was a year or more before she stopped to catch her breath among so many jobs, and noted down that people at Lasky worked so hard she had begun to believe in unions! After a few upheavals and strikes, jobs did become defined and separated. Shooting pictures took more time, and more film was shot of every scene. This ended the emergencies when there was just not film *enough*, after shooting finished—due to a director's mistake or a mishap in the lab—and the cutting room would resound with the cry, "Cut to a basket of kittens." (It was held that footage of a basket of kittens could distract any audience from jerky action on the screen, or lack of sense.) Experts moved in and Mother left the cutting room.

Of course she still went on the set and no one got more pleasure out of this than she, especially if there was a lot of action—best of all, if it was her own. In *The Cost of Hatred*, which starred Theodore Roberts, Lasky's leading character actor, and subsequently an impressive "Moses" in the first of Uncle Cecil's *Ten Commandments*, there had been an exceptionally vicious fight. Mother was amazed (and charmed) at the way powerful, mature Roberts slammed the "juvenile," Tom Forman, over a table and across a room. She was also touched when she read Roberts' lips, moving on the film at the end of the take: "Did I hurt you, Tom?"

She admired Roberts and professionally doted on Forman, who could play the kind of juvenile she loved best to write— unpretty, decent, believable. In *The Cost of Hatred*, he was a young man thrown by fate upon the mercy of Roberts, who proposed to satisfy an ancient grudge through him. The final cost of hatred was that Roberts lost to Forman the one thing

he loved, his daughter—played by Kathlyn Williams, who had been an early Selig star, a little old to pair with Forman, but she had an excellent technique and was the wife of a studio executive.

Mother talked a lot about *The Cost of Hatred*, which she ultimately made into a book *Hands Off!*, an unusual thing to happen then to a screen script. She therefore thought it only fair to let me see it, violence or not. There was an educational aspect, too: the main action had been set in Mexico, and to represent the Roberts hacienda, the director used an historic San Diego adobe, known as "Ramona's Marriage Place."

In her letter to her mother after she had exposed her small but stuffy daughter to the picture, she recorded her surprise. *I thought she* (me) *would pity poor Tom Forman who is so dreadfully abused. Not a bit of it! She actually shed tears over the poor daddy—the utterly brutal Mr. Roberts—whose bad daughter went away and left him.* When Mother ventured to suggest that Mr. Roberts did treat the boy pretty roughly, I replied (she alleged) that he was a bad boy, who had disobeyed his own father (which was true) and deserved to be whipped. Also, I pointed out that the boy had tried to kill himself (as a result of such rough treatment) and this was against the law.

I suspect my severity was one part boasting (I must have just learned that suicide was against the law), one part pure contrariness, and one part the lack of ever having been whipped.

Mother called this the most perfect piece of feminine logic she had come across. Because the boy in desperation tried to hang himself, due to the whipping, the whipping had been justified! I think she was glad to get away from me, back to a straight-thinking (chiefly masculine) world.

While she liked Tom Forman best of the young actors for whom she wrote, she also became fond of Wallie Reid, whom she considered very modest for a star. She was only really

exasperated with him once, when he brought musical instruments to the set, where her script *The Hostage* was shooting nights during summer heat, and created an infernal din till break of day. She worked on *Thirty Days*, his last picture before he died—one of Hollywood's first and most famous victims of drugs.

Best of anything, she liked being with the crew, a craftsman among mutually respecting craftsmen, weathering emotional storms which in a single day could include Wallie's wife having a baby and Fannie Ward having a tantrum.

A few weeks before the tantrum, Fannie had had to put off acting, because of a strained back. A motion-picture magazine, which hadn't hesitated to refer to a Latin American state as a "spiggoty republic," also took advantage of the freedom of the press to ascribe Fannie's ailment to a fracas with her spouse. Now Fannie had walked off a set.

Scouts, messengers, ultimatums were flying back and forth, Mother said. Late in the afternoon she went to talk to George Melford, the director concerned, found him with his cameraman and assistant, *and we gossiped about Fannie et al. like a pair of schoolgirls.* The best of both worlds! *He treated me to lemonade in a thermos, laced with absinthe,* she went on exuberantly. (*I don't like it. It tastes like cough syrup.*)

Fannie didn't come back to the set and Mother wasn't really sorry. That was one less female for whom, being female herself, she might be called upon to write. The money men kept seeing her gift for violence, as in *The Cost of Hatred*, and trying not to believe it. Surely a woman named Beulah Marie Dix would *want* to write for a star named Mary Miles Minter?

Mother puffed her cigarette.

She was assigned to work for one of the unique actors of that time, Sessue Hayakawa.

XIII

Famous Boys

We thought a lot of things about our Hollywood were unique. Out beyond the end of the Boulevard, in the khaki hills, there was a strip of road that seemed bewitched. You drove into it, you shut off the engine of your car, and you rolled uphill.

It was an optical illusion, of course. Just the same, when out-of-towners had had their look at oranges growing on a tree, a movie star, a studio, and the Pacific, we showed them Magnetic Hill as an added wonder, and they never failed to be amazed.

Then there was another wonder in our world—boys, at the Hollywood School for Girls.

Whether Mrs. Woollett really had plans towards a mixed school, or this just happened, has been lost in the mists of history. Marriage had bestowed on her a ready-made family of two girls and a boy; perhaps this gave her an idea. At any rate, boys infiltrated the school, rather intermittently and at the bottom grades, where it was believed in those days that sex didn't matter much.

When I first trotted up the macadam to the primary room where pretty Miss Bemis spoiled the good impression she was making on me by requesting me to spell my name—*No, not Leaf, dear* (and to my chagrin I could not spell Evelyn, although I hated Leaf)—a few boys were strewn among the chucklers. Two I already knew—angel-eyed Billy Buckland

Famous Boys

and dark-haired Jesse Lasky, Jr. Billy lived four or five blocks away from the school in a house his art-director father had designed, with a two-story living room full of shadows at the top and laughter lower down. Jesse, Jr., lived even nearer H.S.G. We also had another Jr., Douglas Fairbanks.

While Billy's father was prominent and Jesse's father was important, Doug's father was a *luminary*. Only little Charlie Chaplin and still littler Mary Pickford loomed as big, though Douglas Fairbanks, Sr., hadn't been a luminary for *too* long. Back East he had played the heroine's brother in Mother's *Rose O' Plymouth Town*.

Shortly after I arrived at H.S.G., the primary classes gave a performance in which Douglas, Jr., had the lead, though not the title role—it was called *The Wild Rose*. Doug played Prince Bumblebee. What a splendid choice! Not only did he act the bee with skill, but since he was a portly child, he was a real Presence around which we garden flowers swayed and bowed. We were horticultural snobs who wouldn't let the Wild Rose join our garden, whereupon she won Prince Bumblebee.

Soon after this, Doug, Jr., must have buzzed away. I remember nothing more of him till I was ten. By that time, Mother had decided that I ought to fence, not (at least that's what she said) because my father had been agile with the Schläger and the sabre, but because it was a tenet of the stage that mastering the foils gave grace. If you were thin, inclined to darting like a dragonfly—but the only shimmer about you was the new retainers (which we called braces) on your teeth—you could use some grace.

Possibly for related reasons, Doug, Jr., and Billy Buckland began fencing, too. We had the same teacher, so one afternoon I was invited to the Bucklands' with my gear. The tall living room had almost as much space for swordplay as a Buckland set, but I made meagre use of it. Terrified not of the blades but of the boys—I was at a boyless level of school then—I clattered blindly through my bouts.

Long afterwards Billy told me that the boys had been terrified of me. Maestro Brigandi had assured them that I was a youthful female Anglo-Saxon Cellini with the foils. It was just to goad them. Bibi, bless her heart, had done much the same, boasting of me to her grandchildren—and I didn't know about that till later, either, nor understand why sometimes they were slightly cool to me.

The next appearance of Doug, Jr., for me and H.S.G., was across the fence from the big pine, when I was at the stage now known as junior high. Doug's mother took a house that backed against the school. Never had that batch of green benches been so popular for lunch. Girls nearly choked getting down their peanut butter sandwiches so their mouths would not be full in case there came a chance to smile at Doug, at a window. There was also a swing on which, if you didn't mind the risk of swinging over the top bar, you might pump yourself to window height.

Of course, Doug was no longer stout. He was trim and elegant (fencing?) and on his own way to a theatrical career —also, when he still was very young, to romance, but not with any H.S.G. girl. After a much-publicized courtship, he married Joan Crawford, then a symbol for most people of the Charleston trimmed with rhinestones. Not the partner, much of Hollywood clucked, for the sensitive and bookish Doug.

Veda Buckland disagreed. Joan was *wonderfully* sensitive, she said, simple and sincere. Far from really living like her gaudy image, she liked going without any make-up at all, taking pensive beach walks alone, and spending quiet hours among books. She and Doug were happy at the Bucklands', evidently, but not happy enough otherwise. The marriage didn't last. He finally moved to England, to become even trimmer and more elegant.

He made several pictures first, among them one from a book Mother and Bertram Millhauser wrote. I had had no chance to see his father in *A Rose O' Plymouth Town*, but I

Famous Boys

did see Doug, Jr., in *The Life of Jimmy Dolan*. The book was filmed twice. The second time (*They Made Me a Criminal*), John Garfield was starred and did seem better suited to the role of a tough, embittered prize fighter than Doug. Still, the appearances of father and son in such widely separated works by B. M. Dix gave a nice book-end effect.

Then we had a famous boy at H.S.G. who wasn't in the lower grades. This came about because of The Great Flu.

Up till then we had had pneumonia, grippe, and croup. Influenza was new and, to adjust us to the name, there was an inane joke about a bird called Enza—"I opened my bird cage and in flew Enza." This seemed quite hilarious for a few seconds, in the third grade.

The epidemic was far from hilarious. It swept the East, but didn't miss Los Angeles, either. We endured brushfires, earthquakes, a pair of hellfire-and-damnation pastors, and a touch of Ku Klux Klan, so why not this? Many Angelenos caught the flu and most of them stayed off the streets. When you drove to Pasadena (as we had to once, even in this crisis), you traversed an empty city. The very few individuals outside were like hot-weather Martians (it was very hot) with their white clothes—white being prescribed as germ repellent—and gauze masks.

I did not have the flu (I had an earache), but my father did and was duly quarantined. Mother spent a couple of frenzied weeks tending us both between dashes to the typewriter to complete her script *The Heart of Youth* for Tom Forman and Lila Lee, made from her book *Friends in the End*. It was hard typing in her mask (you were likely to chew gauze along with your underlip), but she was often too rushed to take it off.

Father was confined in an upstairs bedroom. I was not allowed to see him, only to yell at him. Once in a while our Joe Kamemura, festooned with gauze, would enter his room to clean. Joe felt Father must be lonely, and also that it was a

nuisance to wear gauze. He would push back his mask, Mother told me, sit down on the bed, and have a rousing chat with the invalid. There were no ill effects for him, and we wondered if the clouds of incense drifting from his basement quarters helped.

Due to the influenza, schools were closed, but the Hollywood School for Girls came ajar. Back we went to our sturdy white chairs and our scarred white desks (white for the lower grades —brown further up); and some poor-sport parents, who didn't accept this chance for their sons to wander wild and free, shoved them into our high school. One of these sons was Joel McCrea. He was a tall youth with a pleasant smile, though not the brilliant one we basked in later on. Perhaps the brilliance came from the reflection that the worst already had happened to him! It was not going to be easy to have on his record that he once attended a girls' school. Probably it wasn't even easy while he did. Down at my level, the shock of his presence was muted and delayed, but no one between the jacaranda and the castor beans could ignore the extra flutter of notebooks, bosoms, and eyelashes.

With the term ended, Joel was gone. He came into our lives again as the most gloriously tanned, agreeable, and lithe of the many dazzling young men at the Santa Monica Beach Club. Watching Joel leap at the net for a "kill" in volleyball was as thrilling as watching a good surfer catch a wave.

After that, he was in the movies. It would be nice to imagine that his H.S.G. experience encouraged a doggedness that got him through minor roles, that it sharpened the insight which made his performance in *The Primrose Path* so touching and genuine, and helped sustain him so that twenty years later he could stunningly contribute to the re-creation of Westerns and Western types in *Ride the High Country*. It would be nice—and he might be too agreeable to disagree.

No more epidemics with such a happy side effect occurred. No boys, starting out in kindergarten, which met on the lawn,

Famous Boys

persevered to the high school barn. Most often they dispersed by the first grade, perhaps reacting like Jesse Lasky, Jr. According to his cousin Ruth Lasky, on the day he learned to read the sign "Hollywood School for Girls," he climbed across the stone wall and went home for good.

At sixteen, Jesse published a book of verse, *Songs from the Heart of a Boy*. Maybe still afflicted with a childhood trauma, and to make assurance doubly sure, he began one poem robustly, "I light my pipe...."

XIV
Swimming Pools I Have Known

Jesse, Jr., figured in the annals of my Hollywood swimming, too.

If the fjords belong to Norway, if surfing makes you think of the Pacific isles, and the seashore has been a European style since the female ankle was considered moral enough— as well as tough enough—for exposure to the sun, swimming pools by now surely have become a synonym for Hollywood. The swimming pool syndrome, though, was barely beginning back in 1917.

For me, swimming started at Ray Pond in Vermont, not long after I could walk—I got bored with watching adults splash around in the lake and stepped off a float. Down, down I went, obtaining a better vision of how the float was moored to the lake bottom than I really craved, but up, up I came thanks to buoyancy and puppy paddling. After that, it was decided I should be *taught* to swim.

Technique at first seemed to me a good deal of a waste of time, in view of my survival in the pond. I just moved dreamily hand-over-hand along the edge of our Boston plunge (a vigorous, foamy word one never hears any more), until a forbidding lady in an oblong bathing suit hollered down, "That little girl will have to get out if she isn't going to swim." Nobody was going to drift through life in a Boston plunge. They should have been admired if they could. The water was pretty cold.

Swimming Pools I Have Known

This, then, was preparation for the chlorine culture of the future. However, the early pools we knew had very little chlorine—or occasionally much too much. Furthermore, their temperatures were not so far removed from those of Boston or Vermont.

Of course we had the cool Pacific Ocean, too. But though my father once convulsed a youthful audience by describing the Grand Canyon as the biggest ash tray he had ever seen, we didn't quite snub the Pacific by calling it a pool. Neither, according to Mother at least, was it a place where you could truly swim, what with the breakers. I had to agree with her, at least when I was six.

It was the Jesse Laskys who introduced us to our first Hollywood pool. They lived in a big white house with a tiled roof, of the kind we then called Mediterranean. A few years later, stucco walls were built to look hand made, window space increased, arches opened everywhere, and California-Spanish architecture was born.

The Laskys had a tennis court—I was awestruck on a Sunday when I first saw four men in spotless white, beyond the fence that shut me out, moving so fast they seemed to fly like angels making a go of paradise—and they also had two pools, a big one, and a little one where children could play alone. This was where Jesse, Jr., and I settled down one weekday afternoon when his governess was busy with the new Lasky baby and no tennis was underway. The program for our afternoon did not include swimming. We took off our shoes and socks to get our feet wet while sitting on the edge.

Then I had a wonderful idea, the dawn of a bent towards gymnastics on which the sun immediately set. I would get up, step out from the edge of the pool, bend at the knees on the way down, and end sitting on the edge again, legs hanging in the water. I stepped out—but I didn't bend and found myself standing in water to my waist. Jesse and I were taken aback. Neither of us welcomed a mishap which the adults would want

Explained. I don't know whether he thought he might be accused of pushing me, but I know I was always inclined to feel blame for *anything*, and we came to a mute agreement not to make a fuss.

For the next half hour, until I was called for by Mrs. Main, a kind lady chauffeur Mother sometimes sent for me, we ran up and down (out of sight of the house) and I shook a lot of moisture off. Anyway, my socks and shoes had not got wet, so there were no damp footmarks in the living room when I went to bid my hostess, Bessie Lasky, good-bye.

Jesse, Jr.'s, mother, Bessie, was delicately pretty, with a light voice which increased a feeling that her toes barely touched the ground. She was versatile, a patron of the arts, and an artist herself. In due course a magazine article about her explained, "She stands on her own two feet, does Mrs. Lasky, and she writes and she paints...." *The New Yorker* took note of the phrase, with the caption, "Won't you sit down, Mrs. Lasky?"

That particular afternoon she was seated at a desk, a charming cameo against the sunset light. Maybe the quality of light prevented her, when I said my thank-you-very-much-I-had-a-lovely-time, from noticing the water trickle off my skirt. She gave me long, polite attention, though, so I must have made a considerable puddle. I often wondered what she thought afterwards. Perhaps, however, with her mind on poetry and paint, she wouldn't have observed a puddle unless she stepped right in it and it squelched.

It was still a must with Mother for me really to swim, so we looked around for places suitable to practicing. The school sent parties of us deep into Los Angeles; apparently there were no suitable public swimming facilities in Hollywood. Transportation was by car pool. One day this consisted only of my father and his five-seater Roamer. Unwilling to disappoint anybody, he loaded in fourteen. The car gave out at Sunset Boulevard and Vermont Avenue, within hailing distance

of the Frank Lloyd Wright house, built for another patron of the arts, Aline Barnsdall. (There was a pool in the living room which Mother looked on as a hazard, if you had a sudden impulse to cross to a bookcase or the fireplace.) Unfortunately, hailing did no good and Father had to walk up a steep hill for help. We got another car, but not that day, and soon the swimming shifted to a handier location, Bimini.

Bimini Baths had a striking advantage over other pools— heat. Its several plunges ranged from the cozy to the sizzling. I could hardly wait to get across the corridor mats (ropey and unpleasant anyway) into a hottish pool where I studied back and breast and side strokes. The Crawl seemed as yet a misguided whim and the Butterfly was nothing but an insect. Finally I would climb into the fountains by which the pools were filled, a perpetual shower-bath cum jungle-gym, and shudder rapturously in the heat while Mother continued her breast stroke, lap after lap with her head up (no bobbing underneath for her!) like a mink.

By the next time I encountered full-sized private pools, I was able to remain afloat not by buoyancy and luck but by plan. I could even go down to the bottom on purpose, now— quite a safari, for you couldn't see a thing. Pools were dark. Today's transparent blue or green, or the grey chiffon of duller weather, were unknown. Pools had a jellied look, if they weren't utter murk. They were drained from time to time but not vacuumed. Who ever vacuumed a swimming hole?

Pools began to abound. Where once our yearning comment on a friend had been, "She's got a doll house," or "She's got a dog," it now became "She's got a pool." After all, you only stared at someone else's doll house and it didn't pay to fall in love with someone else's dog. With far fewer reservations, you could share your neighbor's pool.

The prettiest of the "old" pools I ever knew belonged to my classmate Helen in the Wilshire district, a select part of Los Angeles when Beverly Hills wasn't much more than open

range. Helen had long hair (red—we were almost *not* a minority at H.S.G.) and what adults called a Botticelli face. I wasn't quite sure about the significance of this, or of the Remington drawings she showed me at her father's house—it was quite an arty afternoon—but I did appreciate the picturesqueness of the pool.

Walking through the dusky house (blinds drawn against the sun—this was no cabana!) with your feet bare on the Persian rugs, you could drop right into the water beyond the glass doors of the drawing room. High walls enclosed the pool on its other three sides and they were hung with autumn vines which tossed down leaves the shade of Helen's hair. The water may not have been filtered (it was jade), but the effect was as romantic as swimming in the desert, or a pool's length from the snow, at Lake Louise.

Hollywood pools seemed to get trimmed with beautiful women, just as in Hollywood publicity. (I was aware of the beautiful men, too, but I couldn't really gaze at them.) At the Hollywood Athletic Club, which emerged in the twenties as a residence for bachelors, a spot for exercise, and our choice for Sunday dinner, there were three women swimming away who were especially attractive, and another who was attractive and alarming, too.

In the first bracket was Maria Corda, then the wife of producer Alexander Korda. She had come to Hollywood to star in her husband's film *The Private Life of Helen of Troy*. The difference in the way they spelled the name possibly reflected other differences, for they subsequently got divorced and the producer married one of the most beautiful women alive, Merle Oberon. However, blonde Maria Corda, making a stately progress down the pool, was a good deal of a Venus, too.

Next there was Olive Borden, with jet black hair, a saucy nose, a short upper lip, and a figure featured (with veils) in fan magazines. And there was Cornelia Brown, wife of Johnny Mack Brown, the Alabama football star and then movie star.

Swimming Pools I Have Known

She was pretty, delightful, and could dive. Even if you were a fervent Johnny Mack fan, it was impossible after knowing Cornelia to sigh enviously, "Some girls have all the luck." Any movie star would have been lucky to be married to Cornelia.

The alarming girl was Emil Jannings' daughter Ruth. After enormous successes in *Variety* and *The Last Laugh*, landmark European films, Jannings was in Hollywood, and Ruth worked out at the Athletic Club. She climbed up and down a rope. At other moments she harassed the rest of us by barring our way from lockers and performing other feats of strength and skill. One morning she came to exercise with a noticeably bruised mouth. She had been to visit her father's set (*The Sins of the Fathers*), she told us, walked through a door right into Barry Norton—an Argentinean despite his name and the recent co-star of *Mother Knows Best*—and he kissed her hard. That morning Ruth looked as pretty as anybody else.

Length after length, splash upon splash, tan upon tan, those were shining swimming hours—except for a few, and they concerned the most friendly pool of all, Uncle Cecil's.

The pool lay at the base of a slope where, on July Fourth, until Los Angeles became too metropolitan, we used to set off fireworks and hang our sparklers on a cedar tree. By this time Katherine Lester lived with the de Milles. She was an orphan with a thrillingly romantic history (thrilling to me, that is—perhaps not to her), and we saw each other often till she went away to school. The de Milles already had an adopted son, John, and Katherine was in the process of being adopted when I went to spend a night Up At The House, as we always spoke of Uncle Cecil's.

After a stroll with her dog, Patrick Henry, we decided we would like a swim. Due to the cleaning-by-refilling process, pools had a horrid way of being empty when you needed them. This happened to be our case. Better luck tomorrow! We turned the water on.

That night Uncle Cecil was at the studio till late. After

dinner Aunt Constance took Cecilia, Katie, and me to the movies. We walked across the top of Laughlin Park, a square half mile of trees and shrubs originally set out by a pottery-maker from Ohio. At our Boulevard neighborhood theatre, we saw Priscilla Dean in *The Virgin of Stamboul*. Mother made the only comment on photography that I remember, over *The Virgin of Stamboul*. She said she couldn't tell Priscilla Dean from the camels, in one of the close shots. Naturally I had been dying to see *The Virgin of Stamboul*.

It was only on the walk back, in the quiet darkness where you could hear a mountain lion sneeze and notice stars fall, that we thought again about the pool. (Could that noise have been a gurgle?) We wondered out loud if a gardener—or someone —would have turned the water off. Aunt Constance and Cecilia fancied not. Whoever turned a faucet on was responsible for turning it off. That was a law of Persians, Medes, and pools.

We reminded ourselves that the water ran in very languidly. We walked fast and pointed out that there was no use worrying. Aunt Constance mentioned that she hoped the new tennis court wasn't being undermined.

The night was *very* dark and the stars were very bright. As we gasped across the summit of the Park and down to the de Mille lawn, stars glittered on it, too. Water lay across it in a sheet. Katie paddled to the valve, with me right after her. We twisted and tugged. The valve stuck. Cecilia stood apart, her hands—so strong from managing horses—tucked in the pockets of her fur jacket. If anyone thought, she said, that she would ruin her new shoes in all that water, they were wrong.

A moment later, leaving her shoes safely on a rise, she turned the water off. We had only a flashlight to assess the damages. It produced a merry glitter everywhere we glanced. What could we actually do? We went to bed.

Certainly I would have preferred going home, but I had caused enough trouble without asking to be sent or to have someone come for me. I blamed myself. I had known the de

Swimming Pools I Have Known

Milles longer than Katie. I was her guest, and she was filling up the pool for me. Far worse, I wondered if she was on probation in the family. Perhaps because of me she wouldn't get adopted? I didn't really think that of Aunt Constance and Uncle Cecil, but I didn't *know* and couldn't ask.

Up At The House, life was not the way it looked in de Mille films. No bathroom was ornate, and as to bedrooms of splendor and romance, everybody except John—who had asthma—slept on a screened porch. I huddled down in the spare bed next to Katie and wondered how kind Aunt Constance and kind (so far) Uncle Cecil would look at me in the morning.

I woke very early. Katie did, too. Holding our breath, toting our still-damp shoes, we tiptoed from the porch down into the garden to face what had to be faced. The pool lay gleaming as if silver polished, flat as metal in the grass, which gleamed a little, too, but was nearly dry! The tennis court had neither cracked nor sunk. The worst disaster was some slight erosion of a strawberry bed.

Uncle Cecil and Aunt Constance didn't look, or say anything, and Katie stayed Up At The House and grew up the most beautiful de Mille. We swam together many times after that—but not that day. I think we didn't want to displace one more drop of water to the grass. We went to the movies instead and saw desperately exotic Alla Nazimova die in the arms of desperately handsome Valentino in *Camille*, and cried enough to flood another pool.

XV
On a Clear Day You Can See Hayakawa

Down at the corner where Argyle Avenue meandered across Franklin and where, until late at night (ten o'clock), the Dinky clanked around a curve and made a useful stop, there were castles—two of them.

They were really big plaster houses, each with a tower, built by a gentleman who was a bit of an ornament himself. When he took his daily constitutional along the Boulevard, he wore a frock coat, heavy make-up, and a top hat. As from time to time he acted in a movie, this may have been preparedness for his next role, but I always thought he was keeping up the tone of his estates.

He lived in the larger castle, designated as *Sans Souci* on a mounting block I saw used only once. A boy from Vine Street, breathlessly proclaimed by my playmates to be a meatpacking heir—really more exciting than a star—rode his pony down and dismounted on it.

Opposite, in Castle Glen Garry, lived Mr. and Mrs. Sessue Hayakawa. Mother took me to call on them, before she hunched down over her legal pad to complete *The Call of the East*.

Sessue Hayakawa had had great success in a picture Uncle Cecil directed in 1915, *The Cheat*. (In the big scene he branded Fannie Ward for being a tease.) *The Cheat* had started as a play by New York drama critic Hector Turnbull. It finally ended as an opera. Hector Turnbull, a correspondent during

On a Clear Day You Can See Hayakawa

World War I, married the ex-Mrs. Samuel Goldwyn, my friend Ruth's mother, almost as he set foot on the dock on his return from overseas. Driving past the Paris Opera House with Ruth many years later, he told her he had seen *The Cheat* performed there. Operas were rarely made from plays and surely until then never from a motion picture!

In spite of the impact of *The Cheat* and of great dramatic gifts, there was difficulty finding roles for Sessue Hayakawa. The public, known without much tenderness to our movie group as Lizzie and Jakie, asked for love. How could you provide a fade-out with a kiss, with Hayakawa in the leading role? (That is, unless it was an all-Japanese cast, for which there was small demand.) Miscegenation might have been a four-letter word—how much simpler if it had. Even liberal-minded people muttered, "What if there were *children?* . . . Half-breeds."

Dedicated to that proposition that all wars are the same, meaning people are alike, Mother had few prejudices, but she had to work with those that other people had. To appease Lizzie and Jakie she must devise a story that wouldn't seem too sad and a romance that wouldn't shock. In this case, hurrah for half-breeds! Mother made her heroine part Oriental and part white. What else could such a girl hope for but the love of a fine Japanese?

Luckily there was a girl who, though by no means a half-breed, could look like Yankee sweetness combined with Eastern mystique. This was Margaret Loomis, a dancer who had evidently learned from famous Ruth St. Denis to respect and reflect the beauty of the East. Margaret Loomis played opposite Hayakawa several times. In *The Call of the East*, Mother had for villain Jack Holt who, with William S. Hart, shaped the image of the strong and silent outdoor man of the screen, later perfected by Gary Cooper and John Wayne.

Up at Big Bear, where *The Call of the East* company spent some stirring days in July, 1917, Jack Holt told Mother

that he really had been an authentic cowboy—among many other things. It was fortunate for Mother and director George Melford that Jack Holt was tough. This villain was faced with a comeuppance harsh enough for the worst of evildoers—he was threatened with quicksand.

There wasn't any quicksand (very likely just as well) at Big Bear, and a mountain creekbed had to do. The actor had to be fortified with whiskey for a long ordeal. Two Japanese supporting players (in more ways than one) held him by the arms—for hours, according to the script—lowering him in the ooze.

Mother was extremely sorry for Jack Holt, not so much because during shooting of the picture he sustained bruises and welts, a torn ligament, and a sprained thumb, besides exhaustion and cold, but because several times, for authenticity, he had to get back into clothes encrusted with mud the day before.

Sessue Hayakawa took some punishment, too. During a "take" in which he was supposed to lie unconscious, Margaret Loomis suddenly went into hysterics over her own performance and began pounding on what was nearest, which turned out to be his solar plexus. Whether from fabled Eastern stoicism, or international respect for the-show-must-go-on, Hayakawa never flinched.

The "big set" for *The Call of the East* was a Tokyo street laid out on the Lasky back lot, just behind the Vine Street studio. The action was shot too late at night for me to see, but both my parents went to watch and Father was pre-empted to walk through as a tourist in Japan. Another treat I missed (but so did he) was a dinner given by one of those supporting players, Hanafusa, in Little Tokyo.

Los Angeles then had Japanese and Chinese areas, not as defined as San Francisco's Chinatown, but to us as interesting, just because they were a little harder to find. You would glance up from the outline of the Mexican plaza in the city

center and see an oriental balcony jut out, or glimpse a stone lion or a waving paper fish. When the Union Station was built, most of the narrow alleys and the dim warehouses, where, we believed, smuggled-in Chinese slept in crates, were destroyed. But our Little Tokyo still had all its chiaroscuro when Mother, George Melford, Margaret Loomis, and several other members of the cast and crew climbed the steps of what Mother considered, on the outside, as *a slummy-looking place.*

Inside, though, there was a pleasant room opening to a roof garden through some shoji screens. The guests sat on American golden-oak chairs at an ordinary table. They had tea in small cups, without handles, and rice wafers, offered them by Hanafusa (who spoke very little English) and two others from the cast, Kino and Ayoyama. Then they moved to another room where Mother had her first encounter with bamboo shoots and bean sprouts (Joe Kamemura cooked in Western style) and with other unknown delicacies.

She enjoyed the clam broth in a bowl with a lid, but not the chicken with "pickled mushrooms." She and a few other guests elected to eat with chopsticks, which she reported on as not difficult and rather fun. After the fruit and sake (*I barely tasted it as the reaction is said to be rather vicious,* Mother wrote), some women of the household played the samisen and Ayoyama danced. This was the only social contact I knew of in our circle with the large population of local Japanese and Japanese-Americans.

The Call of the East reached the city theatres soon. Margaret Loomis did an East Indian dance between showings. The picture was well-received. *Photoplay Magazine* commented, "Lasky's little group of Japanese-American subjects is ... a daring and faithful treatment ... of new material." The next edition of the new material would be Mother's original for Mr. Hayakawa, *Hidden Pearls,* which was my favorite picture for many years: in it, he concealed three pearls in an incision in his arm, fascinatingly built up with putty.

But meanwhile, that September, Mother had a rush assignment to go back to Big Bear and write *Nan of Music Mountain* just ahead of the camera. One of her letters states, *We've had as many conferences as the warring powers. We begin shooting without a line of script.* This was considered poor practice even then, except with certain comedies which were improvised.

Up at Big Bear, Mother drafted a hundred and seventy scenes in four days which, even though a scene then meant one shot rather than a sequence of them, as it did later, represented quite a stint. She hardly left her cabin at all and admitted she was tired, but she had really wanted to do *Nan of Music Mountain*. It was full of the kind of action that she reveled in.

Nan starred Wallie Reid and Ann Little, who was a genuine outdoor girl. Later she left the screen for real estate—maybe because acting became more confined, inside studios—and she was in business with my father for some years. Former motion picture people came to decorate many other Hollywood professions and lead other Hollywood lives.

Almost all the men of the Lasky stock company appeared in *Nan*. Jack Holt was rumored to be cross as a bear because he was kept out of the cast at the last minute to work for Uncle William de Mille with Julian Eltinge, the celebrated female impersonator. Being on location, Mother missed meeting Julian Eltinge at a dinner party, a great deprivation to me, as I longed to know what he would wear.

It was late in the season for six-thousand-foot Big Bear. Pine Knot Lodge, where the movie companies usually stayed, was closed. Twenty-six men and three women put up at Knight's Camp, where they soon were joined by a dozen horses, brought back from the desert where they worked in wintertime. Mother was concerned about the horses. *This is their third day on the march and the change of altitude distresses them just as much as if they were human. We shall have to let them rest tomorrow.*

She added thankfully, with regard to her script, that she

had a good, clear book to go by and the author, Frank Spearman, who had stopped in for a look, liked what she was doing. George Melford now let her leave the camp so she could watch the shooting again. Till then he had been afraid she might fall on the rough trails, break an arm, and be unable to write. She found the forest unusually beautiful, despite the cold, and the company, perhaps because of it, unusually close. The food she dismissed as very bad, except for Sunday when cowboy Jack Hoxie, who was to become a Western star in his own right, cooked up marvelous beans with peppers, onions, and bacon.

On the last Sunday, the cowboys "got frisky" and *chapped* some of the crew.

Chapping, as Mother detailed it, was spreading a victim across the back of someone who knelt, *then you scientifically lather said outspread man with a pair of heavy leather riding chaps ... just where it is likely to do him the most good. The cowboys usually initiate a man in this fashion into cattle camps, and they do it now in all Western pictures.* George Melford had had his initiation (twelve strokes, which he termed no joke) years before.

This time there was no present-a-day for me in Mother's absence. I was getting older and there were also getting to be too many absences. But Mrs. Borrodaile was back to see that I did not become too frisky myself, and I had my portion of the wilderness—nature walks. They were not the same as rambling with Mother. Neither was it like the exercise taken by The Hikers, some of Mother's women friends who walked on Thursday afternoons for the sake of their figures as well as their souls—and then met their husbands at cocktails, to regain what weight they had slogged off.

My nature walks were a serious commitment to the creatures and plants of Holly Springs Canyon, a delightful gulch just above the Boulevard, which was soon submerged by the lake created for Hollywood Dam. My nature walks instructor

was one of the most remarkable and beguiling of the remarkable people who sooner or later filtered through Hollywood—Opal Whiteley. She was to be a sensation within a year when the *Atlantic Monthly* published a journal she allegedly wrote at the age of six. That summer she was financing her own publication of her book *The Fairyland Around Us*, by means of the nature walks.

Opal Whiteley grew up in a lumber camp, loving living things. (Thanks to her, I saved about a hundred lives—I released a batch of pollywogs I found trapped in a bottle in the Canyon, by the stream.) Whether she was also, as she later suggested, a daughter of Henri of Orléans, pretender to the throne of France, no one seems quite sure. He had died in 1901, after an extended nature walk of his own, discovering the sources of the Irrawaddy.

One story had it that Opal Whiteley's mother was Prince Henri's royal cousin. Another was that Opal was a granddaughter of the ruler of Udaipur. In fact, she is believed later on to have lived for some years in the palace at Udaipur as the Princess Françoise Marie de Bourbon-Orléans.

Hollywood has had both royalty and imposters. That summer in Holly Springs Canyon, it had a brunette elf who made the rocks and thickets as exciting as a fairy tale. She inspired us with admiration for the trap-door spider and the rattler, along with emotion for the dogwood, breezes, and the dew. What did it matter whether she was part East Indian or part hoax? Her eyes were so lovely, so intense—and so East Indian, too, though the Whiteleys in Oregon disagreed.

Again there was a reservation in my pleasure when Mother came back from Big Bear—it meant the end of Indian summer, and the end of nature walks.

XVI
Being Bad

Sometimes with me there was more than just a tendency towards being frisky—I was *bad*.

Not when Mother was away. There was a gentlemen's agreement that I would be good then. This appeared to reflect a pair of family commandments: "You don't talk behind somebody's back" and "You don't hit some one when he's down." At Big Bear, Mother was up but, as a parent, pretty helpless.

I knew what being good meant. At my birthday party, when I was four, I had a heady triumph. My cousin Harrabee Larrabee (her given name was Harriet and her middle name was Larrabee) slapped my face as she said good-bye. I had done nothing noticeable to deserve this. Perhaps as the result of Sunday school—more likely from an unreligious shock—I did not slap back. My grandmother (I was her sole grandchild) was excessively puffed up, and I basked in a self-righteous glow for weeks.

That was being good. Being bad I wasn't quite so certain of. Oh, the big things I understood, Mother's major commandments—you never betrayed a friend, or harmed an animal, a child, or someone old (in that order, I presume), you never lied, you never stamped your foot. (You also never cheated at exams, an extension of lying, but I didn't have them yet.) When it came, however, to walking first through a doorway, failing to look people in the eye when you were introduced—though for

some reason you did *not* look waiters in the eye—and talking with your mouth full, matters got more complex.

At an early age I struggled to pinpoint villainy. About the time at which I composed my first and finest verse (*A princess lived across the sea / But oh, she will not marry me*), inspired by fairy stories, I also gave a little zip to the narration with which I soothed Mother while she put me to bed. I invented a villainess. Her name was TarTar, after the most disagreeable thing I knew, tar poured out in surfacing the street. TarTar's loathsome crime was snatching back her glass while somebody was filling it. There really was a dark, hard underbelly to my imagination.

By the time I got to Hollywood, I was capable of being a villainess at first hand (TarTar never made the trip) and my dreadful act was to spoil a calla lily.

Just back of Bibi's house, around from the geraniums, across from a loquat tree, a clump of lilies grew. I had seen Easter lilies in the East, with their petal fringe, but never anything like these, densely white, silk-velvet smooth, with unbelievable pistils of plush gold. There was something irresistible about the thought of what a lily would look like without a pistil, and one afternoon I nipped one out.

While it would be easy to term this Freudian, I had no such frame of reference. Base, destructive curiosity was my whole compulsion, a compulsion that seemed flimsy indeed when I held the pistil in my hand and couldn't put it back. I did try. Askew, it only pointed to the crime. I think I buried it. The assaulted lily swayed on with the rest, smoothly hollow as my drinking mug, while I mooned round the house waiting for the voice of doom which would announce discovery.

Nobody had ever beaten me. The worst that had happened corporally was that Mother smacked my legs when I lost my temper back in Waban and once shut me in the bathroom (*never* in a dark closet) to yell myself out. Yet, because of instinct or habit, or perhaps love, I couldn't bear Them to be

Being Bad

angry with me—Father, who could be quite sharp; Mother, who would be disappointed; Bibi, who, with supreme tact, never stepped in like a parent, yet never backed away.

So I braced myself for whatever combination of contempt and hurt would be accorded me. Nothing happened. Nobody, presumably, glanced at my empty lily. Being a born sobersides, instead of taking this as an encouragement to further evil, I considered it a narrow squeak and left other lilies alone.

Still, I *needed* to be bad occasionally. Mother found me on the stairs one day, when she came home from work, repeating all the awful words I knew, one of which was *awful*. She asked for a list. I provided *wicked, horrid, vicious, nasty, gosh, darn*, and even *damn*. Mother continued on up to the second floor hurriedly and sounded as if she might choke on the drink she poured herself from our Holly Springs water cooler.

The next result was to make her realize that I had some unused energy, so when I asked if there could be one day every year when I might do anything I wished, she cautiously agreed. She knew pretty well what that would be—Frowned On things like eating jelly beans and looking at the comic strips.

The day I selected for my fling was unfortunately one Naomi Myrick's family had picked for an outing. Naomi, who had lived across the street, now lived across the fields on Vine Street where her family kept chickens next door to movie actors and directors. I had planned my freedom round Naomi, who was a bit older and less supervised than I. To make the best of a bad situation, she agreed to hang a string from a window near her bed, having tied the string to one toe. Arising at the crack of dawn, I would climb the hill, tug the string, and she would come out to play before her parents and her brothers woke.

I overslept.

When I panted past the hen houses, causing a racket that was taken up by local dogs as far off as the Boulevard, the Myricks had left for the day. All alone, I removed my shoes for the ordinarily forbidden rapture of walking barefoot "like

the other kids." The bare ground hurt and the sidewalk was too hot. I put my shoes back on and forged up another hill, normally out of bounds, hopping from rock to rock. "Like a mountain goat," I commended myself, and promptly fell and skinned my knees, which was nothing new. I ate so many jelly beans I never looked at them again, riffled the comics, and went back to folklore illustrated by Arthur Rackham and N. C. Wyeth.

My family may have been sorry for me and my meagre revolt, for on Sunday, though it was too hot and not what they'd had in mind, they decided at noon to take me to the beach. Anything was ideal beach weather to me. I collected my blue bathing suit, my beach hat, and my pail, all of which I was outgrowing. I had come to an understanding with the sun and, redhead or not, was getting tanned.

Just as we were at the door, the Reichers dropped in. Ordinarily I adored the Reichers, thin, blade-like Uncle Frank, purring, plump Aunt Ella. What monsters they looked now! It was after one—the beach day was washing out to sea!

My parents welcomed them with open arms. Coffee? Tea? I opened my mouth for an appropriate remark ("We are on our way to Crystal Pier") and was shot down. *Go and see if there is any of Joe's puff pastry.* At a time like this? Wasn't this harming a child, and betrayal of a friend?

Not in my parents' view. Maybe it was not only being cheated of the beach, but a sense of second place, which swept me to my room and under my bed to kick my heels. As I had on shoes (of course), I attacked the floor with a satisfying whack. There was quick response. Mother arrived and in her clearest, lowest tone made it plain that I was verging on the unforgivable. Hospitality, I learned, was a higher law even than a promise given me. It would never be my favorite law, but I did quit kicking. Anyway, my heels had begun to hurt.

I had bad luck with the floor in general. A few years later I became a week-night boarder at the school to toughen me up for

Being Bad

a trip to summer camp. The Main House seemed a little bleak after the student body as a whole went home. I felt ill-at-ease with the regular boarders, like a mere prison researcher among prisoners. Their parents were miles away, or fraught with difficulties. Mine were down the street, minus big problems, ready to pick me up on Friday night.

Things got better when the youngest boarder began to follow me from room to room, asking questions. Flattered, I made up a question game. I was an oracle. An oracle must have a cave. The cave prospects upstairs in the Main House were slim. I chose the space beneath a chiffonier, and crawled part way under, which was as far as I would fit. The posture inspired, alas, just about the wisdom one might expect. My little friend's questions sounded so much smarter than my replies that when she suddenly tossed out, "Why is Helen's mother homely?" my only thought was to get speed, if not wit, into a riposte. "Because she puts on so much make-up," I rapped out.

Make-up was a lively issue then around the school. Girls of ten or twelve had been suspected by Mrs. Woollett of dabbling in powder, while the *old* ones, in the fullness of their teens, actually brandished lipstick just a foot or two outside the gate. Mrs. Woollett gave us passionate speeches on cosmetics, which she denounced with the fervor of a teacher nowadays denouncing Pot. How she loved our dear little shiny faces! she would wind up, an impressive argument if the object of any fifteen-year-old girl had been to achieve her woman principal's love.

So a reference to too much make-up seemed to me an excellent oracle response. Needless to say, it winged straight from beneath the chiffonier to Helen, and there was a great To Do. Neither she nor, to my chagrin, my parents were the least appeased by my explanation that it was a *game*, and that both Helen and her mother ought to be aware I didn't know what I was talking about. (I had glimpsed Helen's mother only once, she was pretty, and I hadn't the least inkling as to whether she used make-up or not.) According to my father at his sharpest,

you did not use actual people as the raw stuff of make believe.

I was stupid to have thought I could. Still, I was nine—and a full-grown studio, not too long after that, paid a fortune in damages for having put into a film its own make believe about a duchess assumed dead, but who turned up in court alive and indignant at their version of her.

My guilt complex throve, proceeding from I-do-everything-wrong to If-anything-is-wrong-I-must-have-done-it, until finally I confessed to a crime I did not commit. Our sixth, seventh, and eighth grades were packed into a single room. The class that was to recite moved to the front. This meant a lot of slithering from desk to desk. On one desk I visited there was a piece of decorative bark. I wanted terribly to see if it was soft, and though a most important family rule was Don't Touch, I stuck a pencil point into the bark.

When our room teacher opened the session following recess with the solemn statement, "Somebody has done a dreadful thing," I was so overcome I never heard what else she said. I followed her from the room at noon and told her I was to blame. She looked surprised. Ernestine, a ravishingly beautiful girl who pouted through lower school because Samuel Goldwyn had seen her on a train when she was twelve and suggested she should act (and her family had held her back), overheard my confession and apology.

Ernestine didn't like me—perhaps because she knew my father was her family's friend and agreed with them about the acting. "Of all the disgusting things," she burst out, "to take a ruler and smash somebody's chocolate fudge cake!"

Me?

I discovered that the eighth graders had brought cakes for an after-school sale, and the very richest one had been found mashed flat on a cloakroom table. *But I didn't....* Just try and explain!

After that I stopped confessing quite so fast, but I still didn't always keep my mouth closed till I knew the facts. Once, unexpectedly, this paid off.

Being Bad

In the spring of my last year at H.S.G., Margaret de Mille and I ran into each other at the beach after she had been away for quite a while. Same old Margaret, I thought—bristly. Dressing after a swim, I remarked to someone that she seemed stuck-up. I was told she needed all the defenses she could get. Her parents were at the brink of a divorce.

A *divorce?*

The Douglas Fairbankses had been divorced some years back. But we had no social life with them and besides, Douglas Fairbanks married Mary Pickford afterwards. Could you quarrel with the pairing of the two biggest stars on any screen? Ruth Lasky Goldwyn's mother also had been divorced. It happened before I knew Ruth and was easy to ignore. The William de Milles were here and now. How would I feel if my parents didn't get along and were separating? Just about as if the world had snarled *Get off.*

For the first time I saw that a girl about my age, and much like me (we had shared a cheerfully futile crush on screen star George O'Brien), might have something on her mind besides one-piece versus two-piece bathing suits. I experienced the impure passion of remorse. Margaret and I really became friends.

XVII
Paradise

Was it any kind of omen that in the early Hollywood days, Paradise burned down?

This Paradise was little advertised—it was Uncle Cecil's ranch, hidden in the hills across from Domremy. Safe from sight-seers and uninvited callers, it was not, alas, immune from fire. During the heavy rainy season of 1916, bridges had washed out—much of our sight-seeing that first summer took us on detours into the beds of dry arroyos—and the summer crop of brush was dense, always ready to explode.

The first time I heard of the ranch was when the morning paper carried a picture of its rustic façade in flames. The event made its mark on me, for though brought up not to fear water, tramps, or dogs, I had been sternly warned concerning fire, with distressing tales of New England houses razed to the ground in blizzards. The fire hoses froze and householders in night clothes caught-their-death-of-cold out in the snow, wretchedly illustrating that old saw we found so humorous in the first grade, *which would you rather have, a hot stake or a cold chop?*

California brush fires didn't give a choice, piling heat on heat as they roared through the chaparral where no hoses stretched. Looking north from the newspaper that morning, I could see the puffs of smoke beyond our hills, and smell it on the unpolluted air. That Paradise was gone before I visited it,

Paradise

but it was rebuilt. Soon my mother, not so much my father, was a frequent guest.

Paradise was a retreat where Uncle Cecil could forget the demands made on him as the Lasky Director General. But it was also a place for concentrating on demands. When Mother was scenarist on a de Mille picture, she was subject to a last-minute week-end invitation for the purpose of story talk. Suddenly on Friday, rolling up an evening dress, she would be off for two days of back-country plot and character discussion. Mother didn't really much like working with Uncle Cecil. His approach to stories wasn't hers, and she preferred him as a dinner host or guest, but he ran the studio, and working with him was a Command Performance.

One week-end invitation caused confusion. My parents had asked an English newcomer to dinner Saturday. He telephoned that morning to confirm the time, and my father told him, "Beulah went to Paradise, but we want you to come over anyway."

"My dear fellow, I wouldn't dream..." the Englishman broke in. "Deepest sympathy." It took Father several moments to explain that "went to Paradise" was not a Western euphemism like "gone to that Great Roundup in the sky."

Paradise, then, was primarily a business spot, to my mind. Other hints crept into the unending local gossip, but for my part I knew of no Wild Parties there. One man's Bible class, perhaps, can be someone else's brawl.

I enjoyed the little that I knew, especially a story Uncle Cecil told about a frog which lived in one of the toilets at the ranch. Paradise had plumbing, though plainly of a somewhat woodsy sort. He told the story so well that though at eight I was depressingly refined, I laughed until I couldn't stop.

The toilet had been consecrated to the frog. In a private porcelain pond, the small creature reposed till, with a nearly godlike operation of the distant tank handle, a cascade was released. Then, Uncle Cecil said, the frog would gallantly

meet the challenge to his strength, stroke through the waterfall, and surface in triumph as the waters fell back, tingling no doubt with froggish satisfaction (which at that point I felt Uncle Cecil and I shared) to the webbing of his toes.

I did not actually visit Paradise until after the frog had gone. Paradise was not child oriented, but as we grew somewhat older, Katie had the premises for an outdoor birthday party. It was held around the pool, a broadened stretch of mountain stream remote from the house. There were already bathers in the pool, Katie explained: two horsehair snakes lived at one end. Around us surged the live oak, lilac, laurel (and poison oak), which had survived the fire long ago or doggedly grown back.

We put on our bathing suits and started to get wet. The pool was cold as an unlit iron stove, colder than unheated city pools, for when the water flows in California, it flows quickly from the snow. We splashed a lot, in the end far from the horsehair snakes. They never stirred except with the movement of the stream. They may have been cold, too. Or maybe they were weeds, and there is no such thing as horsehair snakes.

Illusion (if that is what it was) occasioned another Paradise anecdote when Katie was well in her teens. Paradise by then had both a main house and cottages. On a family week end, she dashed from her cottage at dawn, without stopping to dress, to wake her best friend, Natalie, with some urgent scheme. It was hot so Katie had slept with nothing on. Natalie, equipped with twenty-twenty vision, even aroused from sleep, (she was to become a costume-designer on half-a-dozen Cecil de Mille films), pointed out a gardener at work across the lawn—Katie couldn't have helped but cross his line of view.

"That's all right," Katie said, "he knows no English," and ran back to her cottage—invisible.

The second trip I made to Paradise was for a wedding. Mitchell Leisen, who began in pictures by designing costumes (he was Natalie's mentor), then designed sets, and then became

Paradise

a director on his own, was the groom. All of us in our teens thought him the most witty, cultivated bachelor we knew. It was glamorous to be there at the wedding, so glamorous that I felt dazed, and remembered from it only that he gave his bride a house key in solid gold.

The idea suited Paradise, for at the heart of Paradise there was a treasure-trove. On the grown-up week ends, Saturdays before dinner, gifts were served. Women guests would choose among pretty objects on a tray. The order of the choice was reached by lot. I thought the custom both luxurious and thrilling—much more fun even than punchboard chances for prizes, a new pastime for us then. The prizes were far nicer, certainly.

When Mother got home from a week end, glassy eyed after a dusty drive and all that story arguing, I could hardly wait to hear about the tray. She might display an evening bag, which had been her prize but—not addicted to *things*—she seldom kept in mind what other women took. In general, I learned, the tray held lovely silk stockings (this was decades before nylon), earrings, combs, and other trinkets. Mother had heard that Uncle Cecil, student of psychology, sometimes tossed in an object of real worth. I have no idea if this was true or whether, if it was, the object ever became recognized.

One Sunday Mother brought home rhinestone shoe buckles and the only personal compliment that Uncle Cecil ever offered her. He had told her she had pretty feet. She was pleased. A theory grew up that Uncle Cecil, connoisseur of women's beauty, was especially a connoisseur of legs and feet. Certainly this much was fact—that Julia Faye, whom we saw so often Up At The House and who played so many leading roles in his films, though she didn't have a beautiful face, had magnificent legs.

Mother never wore the buckles. Reared till she was fourteen in "sensible" flat-heeled semi-boots, she always suffered miseries in other gear. The buckles, representing a short optimism, waited in a drawer till she would feel brave enough for misery

again. Nothing could slam shut for me this new vision of an Ali Baba's cave.

At the end of the teens, Ali Baba's cave came to me.

Cecilia de Mille was to be married, with her cousin Margaret, her half-aunt Nancy, Katie, Natalie, and myself in the wedding group. The sun looked as if it never meant to set on Hollywood or money, then. We had bridal showers every day—lingerie, linen, bathroom (bring a frog?), kitchen, crystal, and then even stockings and handkerchiefs. Julia Faye gave a pajama shower. Jeanie Macpherson gave the handkerchief one, in a suite at the Ambassador Hotel, with elaborate tea and songs rendered by a light-opera star who had recently performed *The New Moon* on our local boards. Finally, after fittings of our orchid satin dresses by the famous dressmaker Irene, came the Bridesmaids' Dinner. We all looked exhausted except Cecilia (who looked marvelous) as the celebrated tray was passed.

The dinner was in Laughlin Park, not at Paradise. The effect was much the same. Among seven girls, I had the second choice. It was hard to decide between a minute white-gold envelope with a minute ruby stamp, on a slender chain, or a gold and onyx ring. But Father had impressed on me a commandment about making up your mind (he would give you two minutes only with the largest unknown menu), and I took the ring. I was motivated by an out-of-character practicality, conscious that the bracelet would start me on a costly career of adding charms.

The practicality proved wise. The Depression was across the room, just outside the portico. Relatively soon afterwards my bit of Ali Baba's treasure was converted into a week's room rent at a brownstone in New York and a bang-up eighty-five-cent meal.

It seemed too bad to give it up, of course. That had been a handsome wedding and a charming ring. But the glamour of the tray and the magic of the ranch can still be worn.

XVIII
Fly with Harry Houdini

Up in the tallest part of the sky, over Mount Hollywood, we sometimes saw an eagle. From Lookout Mountain we might look out at a hawk or two. The owls were below in Laurel Canyon. Butcherbirds came down to Argyle Avenue, and Naomi warned me never to leave my parakeet Tony outside, even in his cage. The butchers would get him right between the bars!

In 1919, airplanes, too, moved through our sky.

The war had ended, not with one Armistice, but two. Naomi and I celebrated the false one just as earnestly as the real one a day later on. We dressed up in bunting and Christmas tree tinsel and struck poses in a vacant chicken yard, which was the best arena we could find, with all the parents and neighbors we could recruit as our audience.

The World War I fliers, not yet celebrated in the movies *Hell's Angels* or *Wings*, came home with their experience and skill. Uncle Cecil, busy though he was, decided to diversify. He opened the first local, commercial flying field. Father quit oil to serve as vice-president and acting manager of Mercury Aviation.

For me it was as exciting as the war, and more immediate. While I had vaguely sensed some of the noble feelings attached to "overseas" and Over There, the Mercury fliers were right overhead. When they descended to earth they were almost as exciting as the flights they made. They had titles—Captain,

Lieutenant, even Colonel—which we still used, though they had been mustered out, and their clothes still looked like uniforms. Since I couldn't call them young in my sense, or old in my parents' sense, they moved with an age of their own, as well as their own speed, which even on the ground could be intimidating.

We all believed a legend that one of them drove from the Hotel Alexandria in the center of Los Angeles to the Hollywood Hotel in the heart of Hollywood—heavy 1919 traffic all the way—picked up a briefcase, and got to the Mercury Field, a distance of eleven miles, in ten minutes. To keep up the pace, Father had a Duesenberg motor put in his new Roamer. It was alleged to function at a hundred and ten miles per hour.

The Mercury Field lay in open country well south of the Boulevard, in a dirt road area where parties from our riding school got in their galloping. On the way, along La Brea Avenue, the city fathers had scattered trellises with climbing roses. The day I saw a bluebird fluttering above a trellis, I realized even a postcard could come true. The Mercury Field had for me the same unreal reality.

Mercury offered sight-seeing flights (ten dollars), flying instruction, and facilities for making films. Uncle Cecil learned to fly. He looked very dashing in his helmet and, of course, puttees. Jeanie Macpherson learned to fly and looked rather dashing, too. Then Mary Miles Minter learned to fly. She had been a child star of both stage and screen. Within a matter of weeks, she became a grown-up one, to rival Mary Pickford. She, too, had long blonde curls. She was called "the other Mary."

The instructor Mary Miles and Jeanie had was Lieutenant Locklear, a brilliant flier and attractive man. Mary Miles' mother didn't see this as an extenuating circumstance when she found out about the lessons. She raged down to the field and told Father, in detail, what she thought about his letting her daughter risk her life and her career.

The only life lost at the field was Locklear's. Flying alone, he had a fatal crash. Father came home that day, not only

harried, but infuriated. Locklear was gone—and on top of that his female pupils had thronged to the field to mourn with all the vehemence of their training and their temperament.

There was an occasional less tragic accident at Mercury, though *never* with a passenger. Our Captain Kenyon seemed a little accident-prone. He cracked an arm. We went to visit him at the hospital while he was in a cast. Father eagerly looked forward to his return to the field, which was at its busiest. On the appointed day, Father meant to be on hand to greet him, but because of a conference with Uncle Cecil at the studio, he was late.

"Where's Kenyon?" he asked, entering the Mercury office.

"In the hospital," his secretary said.

"Hasn't he got here yet?"

"*Back* in the hospital," was the reply.

"What happened?" Father cried.

She hung her head; she couldn't tell him; he would have to find out from the boys. Greatly alarmed, he rushed out on the field and heard the tale. Captain Kenyon had checked in, early and fit, and happy to be back at work. He glanced at some improvements an efficiency expert had made while he was gone, drank a cup of coffee, and strolled over to the outhouse, some distance away. He stepped inside and lit a cigarette. The outhouse blew up. The efficiency expert had had it washed with gasoline.

Captain Kenyon's injuries were not serious, this time, but the damage to the sensibilities of Father's secretary appeared permanent.

Mercury Aviation wanted to emphasize that flying wasn't bumpy or unsafe, but practical for cargo just as much as passengers. The field acquired a Shetland pony as a mascot. It was taken on jaunts in a covered cockpit, to the indignation of the S.P.C.A. We never thought that flying bothered little Mercury. There were no physical effects from it, and his disposition had been wicked from the start. After I had teased and teased to be

allowed to visit him, I learned he couldn't even be patted anyway—he didn't nip, he crunched.

For my part, I was airborne only once, with Lieutenant Pickup, whose name was certainly encouraging, and whom Father trusted not to stunt. It was funny, looking down on Hollywood from the open plane. All the planes at the field were open, with two sets of wings, till the arrival of the Larsen all-metal monoplane from Denmark. Mother went up on the demonstration flight with the mayor and some other notables. But Uncle Cecil decided that the future of aviation lay in lighter-than-air. Besides, airplanes made no money—not at Mercury. Competitors began to offer cheaper flights, and neither he nor Father felt they could reduce their price and keep passengers safe.

Before the field was closed, there was a final thrill. The climax of the Lasky film *The Grim Game* got shot there. Harry Houdini, the great escapist who could get out of chains and a locked trunk underwater, was then at the summit of his fame. It was time for him to be a movie star. An unwritten law of movies is that an actor always ends facing up to the one thing he has sworn he will not do. Houdini didn't want to fly.

But that was what the picture was about, combining the vogue for him with the vogue for planes.

Houdini not only didn't want to fly, he didn't even want to be in a plane on the ground. A plane had been positioned on the brow of Lookout Mountain so that, once inside, he could be photographed against the sky as if in flight. He looked at the ropes which held it down—there was a breeze—and declined to get in, maybe because he had escaped too many ropes. He was shot simply standing near the plane.

We had all gone up to watch, and I ate a picnic lunch with the Pickups, who told me about their wonderful Chihuahua dog, which unfortunately died after eating mashed potatoes on the sly.

Houdini was a kindly and magnetic man, and we saw him

often. I was wearing bloomers then, which my mother felt were suitable for roughing it, and my hair in a long bob. One day Houdini beckoned Mother aside and begged her, gently, to get "that little boy" a proper haircut and some regular clothes, or I might be marked for life. Mother was touched.

The studio, evidently touched by him, too, went along with his resistance to planes throughout *The Grim Game*. (They could hardly force him, anyway.) The picture was shot to compensate for his addiction to the ground; the climax never would have used the star: the hero had to climb down a rope ladder in mid-air, changing from plane to plane. Doubles were not then so commonplace, but a rope ladder at ten thousand feet was no star's proper place.

The two "acting" planes and the camera plane took off from Mercury Field and headed West, which was towards the beach. At the right moment Lt. "Tommy" Thompson, in the higher plane, began to close the gap between himself and Lieutenant Pickup, in the lower one, so the stunt man could descend. But the stunt man didn't. Somewhere over Beverly Hills he had apparently discovered he didn't like being in the air any better than Houdini. If he hadn't gone up in the first place, there might have been sympathy. Now, it was a take.

Tommy, when he found the action had stalled, moved down closer and closer. Lieutenant Pickup edged his plane up. The rope ladder touched one of his wings. Surely the man would jump! Instead, the wings of the two planes locked.

In his office at the field, Father got a frantic call, "Your boys are coming down." He sprang into the Roamer. That must have been its fastest hour.

Thompson and Pickup had been in tight spots before. (At least they weren't being shot at by guns). They flew for the ocean, holding wings, and just before they reached it, they broke free and made a pair of hurried landings in a field of beans. The stunt man must have been rather badly bounced, but not too badly for—Tommy said—he got up and ran and

was never seen again. As the slightly shaken pilots emerged from their damaged planes, a furious farmer charged them shouting, "If you boys knew the trouble it takes to grow these beans, you would come down some other place!"

Father drove up, about then, to explain there had been little choice. The camera plane waggled its wings and went home with the film.

The movie was duly released, and some years after that Houdini used the final sequence in a vaudeville act. One night Tommy took his wife to see the act and found that after running the clip in which the stunt man faltered and the planes locked, Houdini referred to this as *his* narrowest escape. He then invited members of the audience on stage. Wondering what Houdini's reaction to him would be, Tommy joined the group. The great escapist recognized him at once and, without the flicker of a lash, identified him to the audience as "the hero who saved my life in *The Grim Game*."

Father had adventures of his own, disposing of the Mercury planes. He and Tommy took them to Mexico. Father never piloted, but it was sometimes exciting just to be a passenger on flights like those. Though unheralded and not nonstop, they were long flights for the period and occasionally dangerous. Once, after they had made an emergency landing far below the Rio Grande, they were told they had been lucky not to have set down in the valley farther on. An epidemic had broken out there, following the visit of another plane, and the natives were just waiting . . . !

Since the object was to sell the planes to Mexico, the flights were all one-way. Father would come back by train, through El Paso. He made friends with the Collector of Customs, Zach Lamar Cobb, who had acted for the State Department a few years before when President Wilson was at odds with President Carranza. They were troubled times: in 1914, Zach Lamar Cobb made the headlines, reported kidnapped by bandits from a train near Monterey. Fortunately, he had left the train before the bandit raid.

Fly with Harry Houdini

Things were calmer during Father's year of Mexico, but not much. He got paid for the planes in gold, delivered by the wheelbarrow load, under guard, to his bank. He was given the rank of general, for the sake of protocol in the military hierarchy, but he never felt enough at ease with the other generals to risk winning from them at poker or to join them at a banquet on a jaunt to Guadalajara. (He politely pretended to be sick.)

When he took the train North for the last time, bandits raided it! A film company, enroute back from location, was also on the train. The star was Louise Glaum, ranking close to Theda Bara as a vamp. She became hysterical. Father managed to reassure her, partly because he had been forewarned of bandit raids, partly because he could speak to her in German, also her mother tongue.

Uncle Cecil bought a couple of blimps, then quit the lighter-than-air, too. One of the blimps was sold to Goodyear and became a familiar sight trailing advertising banners over the beach or giving passengers a hawk's-eye look at football games. Father proceeded into real estate.

One afternoon some five years after this, he was back in Mexico at the Agua Caliente horse races. There was a large crowd and a long delay at the Customs Barriers on the return. Hoping for a shortcut, he informed a Mexican official that he had known the late President Carranza. The official replied that he was lucky (shades of the wrong valley!) not to have approached the next official down the line or he might have been shot.

As it was, Father had an extra hour's wait.

XIX

The Montessori Class

In 1920, the year Carranza died, Louise Glaum starred in a movie simply titled *Sex;* Mother recovered from working on the second version of Uncle Cecil's *Squaw Man,* which she felt she botched, and enjoyed making a scenario of the play *Held by the Enemy;* and the Hollywood School for Girls produced a Montessori class.

The Montessori teaching method was a little in eclipse just then, though perhaps only in the West. Mother's cousin, the one who got off to so bad a start through *her* mother's working as a clerk, and then went on the stage, had begun to run a sort of Montessori dame school in the proper New England town of Newburyport. Decades later, she retired with the City Council's commendation for her part in shaping noble lives.

Our Montessori class didn't carry on through decades and was hardly noble, unless in the sense of Rousseau's Noble Savage, the more natural man. We were quite natural that year. We scampered freely through the grounds, our little group of both sexes and mixed ages encouraged to develop creativity and questioning rather than to study grammar and arithmetic.

How this aberration came about—though a small school and rather poor, we were not normally bizarre—is another mystery the Main House never did divulge. Somehow, Mrs. Woollett, the Roman Senator, hired on her staff Leah Press, the Song of the Flame.

The Montessori Class

Not that there was anything political about Miss Press. She was simply dark and vivid, full of her cause, on the barricade for children's rights to an enriching and unfolding youth. She also was a dear. We gradually learned that she derived from New York, for she showed us a booklet of verse written by her New York students. The students had first names like Aurelia and Electra and last names that didn't sound like either WASP or motion-picture families. That was strange, but not disturbing.

Recently, though, she had taught at the School of the Open Gate. The School of the Open Gate?

It was on Krotona Hill, a few blocks from my house, but I never visited it. For me, it, too, might have been in New York. We heard a lot about it, though, in our neighborhood. The pupils took sunbaths! Nude! And the school was co-ed. No, the sunbathing wasn't coeducational, but as the sunbath site was fenced off with boards, and boards had cracks....

Nothing was said on Argyle Avenue, Vine Street, or Franklin, on the subject of the teaching in the school. The nudity seemed quite enough—if the School of the Open Gate wasn't actually dirty (a dreadful word employed to cover things too horrible to think about, which the speaker plainly thought about contentedly), it was surely a very careless place, and for children whose parents had few values.

H.S.G. parents were all-values, I had supposed—and along came Miss Press, lean, lovely as a borzoi, bringing with her a few Open Gate girls—and even boys—to the normally all-female level of the H.S.G. fourth grade. Not, however, bringing sunbathing.

Just the same, we had so many other new things to do that for two whole terms even movies and de Milles almost got excluded from my life.

A large classroom into which you had to step down, between the primary building and the high school barn, became a separate world for some twenty of us. There were others, but not all

at one time. Miss Press' recruitment methods made us quickly subject to change. Some mornings she would arrive with a child we believed she had just met on the street. She could no more fail to offer teaching than she could have failed to offer food. Any child not actually in a class she knew must be hungering to learn, whether aware of it or not.

Some children took quick bites of the Montessori class and left. One of them was Queen Silver, about five, a prodigy at chess, with a trailing mass of tangled hair. Miss Press was committed to disentangling tensions (if not hair) and she plainly felt chess would produce them, at that age. Queen Silver's parents evidently preferred tensions *and* the chess, and the little girl stayed only a few days. Since this was so unmathematical a place, she might have stopped being an inchworm and become a butterfly!

The rest of us were often butterflies and not just because we flitted through the grounds. We girls had classes in expressionistic dancing in a room rented in a house four doors away. We performed to records of MacDowell's *Water Lily* or *To a Wild Rose* or to the chanting of a Vachel Lindsay verse. I already did his poem on the Congo at home and had been rendered anti-Belgian by his description of the sufferings the Belgians inflicted on the natives somewhat prior to the sufferings inflicted on the Belgians by Germans. But in the class the finest poem for eurythmics was "The King of Yellow Butterflies," which gave you a chance to stamp and be as bullying as a Napoleon of the cocoon world.

We also had sloyd, the name then accorded woodworking, and science, in a loft where gentle Mr. Lewis, who lived in an absent-minded professor's cabin near the Cheremoya School, showed us lantern slides of amoebas and dinosaurs, and identified types of rock. He was as interesting as Opal Whiteley and a bit less vehement. The boys mingled with us butterflies, and there was a lot of shoving in the dark as the magic lantern hissed.

The real heart of the Montessori class, though, was

The Montessori Class

Thoughts. Every day we spent an hour having Thoughts. We could stay at our desks, if we were that dull, or go outside among the trees, talk, and even draw. Your method didn't matter, but at the end of sixty minutes you *must* express a thought, long or short, prose or verse, about something you had felt or seen.

There was lots of writhing over this. Not every member of the class was articulate or had any wish to be. Miss Press persisted and she had a formula almost guaranteed to loosen tongue and mind. You picked a subject—any subject, even Hollywood. Then you went at it like this: "Hollywood, Hollywood, I will explain to you." Rhyming "freed up" most of us— you had to be an idiot not to find a rhyme for *you*, and the dullest of us could round such a "poem" out: *Hollywood, Hollywood, I will explain to you. It's where we go to school and sometimes to parties, too.*

There were more unusual subjects and explanations, my favorite of which was composed by a student from Down Under in tribute to Mr. Lewis's lectures—*Pithecanthropus erectus, I will explain to you, He was a man and a bit of a monkey, too.* This seemed to sum up rather well all you really needed to know about prehistoric man.

While most of the class stuck with the formula, rugged individualists branched out. Ruth Lasky Goldwyn (now Turnbull) paid tribute to some roses on Miss Press' desk with, *We each have a mother, And you have not; You grow out of the ground, And we do not. I think it is a shame.* For many years I thought she felt sorry that we didn't grow out of the ground. (Perhaps she did.)

Tom and John, the sons of journalist and author Will Levington Comfort, wrote sturdily about Nature and the elements, though without intense enthusiasm. The verses I contributed clanked with classical allusions. One, endlessly long, began *Wisteria, friend of Hyacinthus.* Ruth asked me later what it meant, and I discovered I had no idea.

The proximity of boys at this age—the mean age was ten

—was a lot more stimulating than it had been down in the first grade. Everybody was in love, at least a portion of the time. Tom rather fancied me, but he was only ten (I was nine), and I preferred John at twelve. John played the field. The greatest moment of that school year was when he chased me down the drive through the bamboo thicket—better than "Run Sheep Run" on our hill!

Not being very smart, I did not get caught. I went home and prayed to Bibi's new Buddha-shaped incense burner (which turned red and nodded its head as it got hot) that when I grew up I would marry John even if I no longer wanted to by then. It must have been the wrong Buddha or the wrong incense.

Tom was the one who asked me out, to a matinee. Mother was a bit taken aback and retaliated by inviting *him*, which enabled her to act as chaperon. We had lunch downtown. Tom appeared in a dark suit (knickers, of course—and what wasn't dark that males wore in those days?), very becoming to his light blond hair. He brought flowers. With my head full of his brother John—or Antonio Moreno, whom I far preferred to Wallie Reid—I was ill-at-ease with the boy in the next chair. Soon after this, the Montessori year and my greatest popular success—several other boys chased me, too—came to a close. I had reached my intellectual summit at six, asking bystanders whether they preferred the Trojans or the Greeks (Mother read me to sleep with *Tales from Homer*), and now I hit my romantic peak at nine. From then on, level—with dips.

There was one celebrity among the boys of the Montessori class—golden haired, fair skinned, beautiful (about six), very likable, and very talented. His name was Ben Alexander. If estranged parents couldn't be brought together on the screen by little Ben, or homes found for stray cats, and warm coats for Apple Women, then indeed things would be wrong with films! He was pre-empted for the high school play, Uncle William's *Forest Ring*, and performed as an elf, along with Irene Mayer's farm boy and Agnes de Mille's fairy princess.

The Montessori Class

Very few child actors grew up into solid acting careers. Ben was one who did. He broke all our hearts ten years later as the young dying soldier in *All Quiet on the Western Front* and, in television, still years after that, he had a long success as "Dragnet's" Sergeant Friday.

The Montessori class, too, got its taste of violence. Some of the mornings when Miss Press was late, vulnerable to so much along her way, the boys found self-expression by tossing lighted matches round our room. Perhaps this influenced Mrs. Woollett towards a decision that self-expression, at our age, could occasion too much heat. Next September, Thoughts were confined to books, recitations were not rhymed. Turning from butterflies to moths, we girls huddled over verbs and long division with a new teacher, and again the boys were gone.

XX
Mother Meets the Censors

When you could read "sex" on a movie theatre marquee, what might not be found inside! The movies were now making too much money to be called merely "cheap"—critics jumped up in the very early 1920s to announce that they were rich and evil. They gave young people Ideas!

By this was not meant that they taught young people to think, even though there were some thoughtful, thought-provoking Hollywood films. No, these Ideas—wrong Ideas—pertained to issues such as drinking, smoking, and driving fast, all of which led to worse! As far back as 1916, a fan magazine had described a woman star as having "sex appeal of a fine and gentle sort." How depraved to associate *fine* and *gentle* with a term like *sex appeal!*

But no wonder such depravity exuded from the screen. Look at the movie people's private lives! Rumor had it that producer Ince got shot on a yacht (at least he did die following a yachting party), while director William Desmond Taylor was brought low in a bungalow, a little closer geographically and professionally to us. He had been scheduled to direct *The Ordeal* from the script Mother was just finishing. Fatty Arbuckle, the great comedian, got into *his* trouble in a hotel, and in San Francisco at that, but the party which ended so badly in a girl's death was tightly knit to Hollywood by the busy needles of the Hearst press.

Mother Meets the Censors

This was scandalous enough, added to the publicized divorces, remarriages, and romances of the motion-picture colony, but the outside world preferred to believe there was far more Hollywood vice than got into print or printed into film. Mightn't it rub off on the audience?

In the beauty parlors nationwide, in the barber shops, it was not the wholesome comedies or zany slapstick that got talked about, but the plots involved with sin, stained with sophistication, and those sirens and seducers working in them —Theda Bara, Mae Murray, Erich Von Stroheim with his clicking heels and monocle, Lew Cody with his worldly smile. Movies took the place of draft dodgers and liquor at the top of the list of Being Bad. After all, the war had ended and the Volstead Act begun. Who was left to be hated by the born haters but the sequined female on the screen demanding right in public, "Kiss me, my fool!" or the movie tycoon in his limousine who presumably had lured her into this.

Perhaps it was too late to rescue Theda Bara, but an effort must be made on behalf of innocent young girls so likely to be dazzled by the thought of limousines and of power over men as to dash from a theatre seat straight to the dives of Hollywood.

Hollywood itself made such an effort. Contrary to what the public thought, it could not absorb girls like change in a slot machine. (Boys in this case seemed to have had more sense; they never came West in such droves.) There weren't even five-and-ten-cent-store jobs for most of the girls who arrived with their hopes, their ignorance, and curls. In 1916, Hollywood Boulevard had been a peaceful street, from Vine to La Brea, with occasional vacant lots between the library, the cafeteria, the florist's, the beauty parlor, the ice-cream parlor, and the "Japanese" store. Four or five years later, it was only four or five times busier.

James Cruze, who had been an actor in *The Call of the East*, now was directing and he made a picture called, simply, *Hollywood*. It was a brilliant spoof about trying to become a

movie star—and did little good in keeping Lizzie back with Jakie on the farm. Hollywood movie wives prepared the Studio Club as a help to incoming girls; the Travelers' Aid turned girls back at stations, when they could. Still the girls flocked in, and the antimovie propaganda grew. Why, the movie capital was far more sinister than Limehouse—and the fans knew about that, thanks to Griffith's *Broken Blossoms*, in which Lillian Gish was a waif only Chinaman Richard Barthelmess was willing to befriend! Too many girls were eager to be just such waifs.

Drastic measures became hinted at. Might the movies, like alcohol, be banned?

Mother had already planned a summer vacation in the East, in 1922. The studio volunteered to pay her fare, if she would speak as much as possible about the good in Hollywood. She agreed. She saw lots of good in Hollywood, and little else. Her attitude about the bad (if it didn't involve harming an animal, a child, etc.) was the same with which she would dismiss a nuisance on the street: you picked up your feet. Naturally the movie people on all sides were human, some of them with sudden wealth, some of them with long-term temperament. They worked hard, extended hours. How much time and energy for immorality was left? Not more than elsewhere.

However, as she and I went East on that long train trip again, she knew her mission wouldn't be an easy one. Playing parchesi on the gritty table top, she forgot to win. (Family commandment: Always play to win.) How would she be able to tell the truth and A) keep it from sounding dull, and B) get it believed? Did the public really want to hear that suave Conrad Nagel, the Lasky star, ushered in a church?

She tried her best. Our vacation rang with a refrain of de Mille good deeds (two adopted children, later three, endless charitable work), Lasky patriotism (leadership in Bond drives), and our cultural and civic assets. Mother counted in

Mother Meets the Censors

Greater Los Angeles, its symphony, museums, churches, theatres, as well as the Hollywood Bowl. I was able to assist with a touch here; it had been so much fun to get up in darkness last spring for the first Bowl Easter Sunrise Service, joining an assortment of de Milles, then with breakfast later at the drugstore, where we met some friends in grease paint on their way to work.

On Easter?

I had over-talked again.

While Mother did what she could for the studio, she could do nothing for herself. To her Radcliffe friends, she was sinking into slime, prostituting her ability, for the screen. She should have stayed an author, even if the book she labored on all year reached a mere few hundred readers (not the millions that a movie could), even if she had to take assignments as an author, too, and not always write books from her pure creative impulse. At least they were *books*.

The realities that we sometimes had to eat, that the *book* business in Boston hadn't guaranteed us this, and that switching careers, for Father, hadn't yet assured our family economy, were never touched. In fact, there was seldom any mention of my father's name. The summer was made up of Mother's friends, Mother's relatives, commenting on how she looked, what she wore, what her movies contained (her friends had never managed to see most of them,) and on the growth and freckles of her child. I might have been a gift from the elves, left in a lettuce leaf. I knew better, though not too explicitly, and I soon resented being fatherless. I began to bring my father into every conversation till he hovered like a Henry George or a King Charles' head.

After speaking at the West Newbury Women's Club, in her black-and-white tassel earrings and her black-and-white checked suit, and at her Radcliffe Twenty-fifth Reunion (lapis earrings, white dress, and a hat with marabou), Mother hustled me

aboard our train for the West. I was glad we lived out there in Sodom and Gomorrah and for the first time in six years, I referred to Hollywood as home.

Whether Mother's crusade had the slightest influence, even among her friends, no anathemas could keep the public from the films. Up in Whitefish, Montana, that winter, a small boy on his first date discovered his girl expected to go to *Lord Fauntleroy* (Mary Pickford) while his heart was set on the serial at the rival movie house. He divided his dimes and they went separately. It was snowing, too. How could you put a stop to fans like that?

If they wouldn't listen to reason, their elders and betters and preachers declaimed, there would be censorship.

A terrible period for studios began, with censors thrusting up like thorns out of the ground and censorship boards flourishing in every town. They held no common standards as to what was execrable. Something banned in Boston might be satisfactory in New York, while, in Little Rock, it could produce an absolute spasm with the shears. Whole scenes got clipped out. If they later were put back, frames and even inches had been lost. The action lurched, painful enough to its originators but —and this was even worse—confusing to the audience. Even Lizzie and Jakie liked to have some grasp upon the plot.

But they hadn't the priority now. Writers, first of all, were forced to try and outguess Miss Marybeth Dayschool, Mrs. Ormond Cityhall, and the Reverend Brimstone, sitting on the Board in Magnus Creek. What was wicked to *them?*

Some things we already knew. Guilt must never go unpunished. Not entirely realistic, Mother felt, but perhaps commendable. There could be no hint of using drugs. She was not so certain about this. No one, naturally, would then have defended them. (Hints that a few stars were addicted were too awful to be gossiped about much. Only Mrs. Wallie Reid was brave enough to tell the truth and try to help with it.) There

could be no hint about perversion, of course; no incest. (Please don't even think the words, seemed to be the tone of Magnus Creek—and, by the way, what do they really mean?) No intimacy, even between man and wife; they could not be seen in the same bed, even a dozen feet apart. No natural processes at all —well, a laugh might be permitted over wet pants, but nobody was *born*. Not in West Virginia.

Hoping to hint delicately that her married heroine was pregnant, Mother believed she found an irreproachable device. The young woman (slender as a reed) stared into the petals of a rose, which then dissolved into an infant face. Horrid! Out!

Mother hated censorship. She had had her own brush with it, back in Boston when *Across the Border* played there, almost ten years before. The authorities objected to the vile language used by a character called "The Man Who Curses." He spoke lines like "By God!" and "Damn your soul!" She found a way to get back somewhat at the censors now in her titles, which the Boards also required to be pure. As a strong pejorative she dredged up the word *scut*. ("You scut! You knew the franchise belonged to Marna's brother!") Webster gives scut's second meaning as "dregs, as of beer . . . a contemptible fellow." The first meaning, though, is "short erect tail of an animal." Had the censors glanced at Webster they would surely have found this, too, very horrid.

Censorship had many curious effects. One occurred presently in *His Hour*, that racy tale by swimmer Elinor Glyn, made into a movie with John Gilbert and Aileen Pringle. The lovely heroine got trapped in dissolute John Gilbert's lair, just where every Lizzie in America most longed to be. Virtuously she held off his heartless advances with a gun, until her arm became so tired she fell in a faint. (Mother wondered aloud, in the Iris Theatre, why she hadn't propped her elbow on a table.) Gilbert, stricken with self-blame, carried her to a couch and then undid the top buttons of her dress to give her air.

In order that this gesture, vital to the plot, should not get slashed out in Little Rock, the dress had been designed with what looked like several thousand buttons down the front, neck to hem. By unfastening a dozen, he exposed her collarbone. This did not deter her, on regaining consciousness, from supposing through such disarray that the deed was done. It all left me wondering why, if you couldn't tell you had been raped, everyone made such a fuss.

XXI
Parties I

Hollywood, Hollywood, I will explain to you.
It's where we go to school and sometimes parties, too.

The censors weren't at all sure that we went to school, but they had no doubt about parties.

I did.

Not only did I never float down from my bedroom at night, à la Borrodaile, over what they would have called a Hollywood Party, I never even glimpsed anything resembling dissipation as they (and I must admit, some movies) portrayed it in 1920, 1921, 1922, and 1923. All I saw were a few cocktails, smoking, a fox trot or two, and cards for penny-ante stakes.

Perhaps there was something else?

If so, it was somewhere else, not with Flebbes, Bucklands, Reichers, and de Milles.

Our society revolved chiefly round de Milles, and unlike what you might expect after seeing the giddy café life in Uncle Cecil's *Affairs of Anatole* or the candy ball in his *Golden Bed*, this meant gatherings of family. Every Sunday there were runnings. We would go to see a current film run either Up or Down at the de Milles', depending on whether we went up to Laughlin Park or down to the corner of Hollywood Boulevard where the William de Milles had a big brown house.

Actually the William de Mille house was not as big as Uncle Cecil's—which was now two houses, the second one known

as The Other House and connected to the first one by a glassed-in walk—but it often had more guests and, as at Aunt Anna's teas, they were prone to be distinguished ones. After a running there, Reinald Werrenrath, a star of the New York Metropolitan, sang us "The Road to Mandalay." Charlie Chaplin did a pantomime. From the front-row cushions where we children sat, he commandeered the girl next to me, Isabelle, to be his partner in the demonstration of a slow-motion kiss. Isabelle was twelve, and shy. Everybody was amused but her.

Agnes and Margaret de Mille soon grew beyond the cushions and had chairs, surrounded by attentive young men. One was dark Arthur Lubin, a promising actor who would turn director, (and, among his other feats, direct the paces of Francis the Talking Mule), and another was blond Douglass Montgomery, a promising actor who would go to New York and be featured with the Lunts. Agnes was by then attending "The Branch." It really was a good little school, its supporters said defensively of the future huge and famous University of California at Los Angeles. Nearly four thousand students were enrolled in 1922.

Margaret was still at H.S.G. where one day another Sunday evening guest, Rollo Peters—who was appearing downtown as "Romeo" opposite Jane Cowl's "Juliet"—came to fetch her, spreading shock waves from the carriage drive.

It was interesting at the William de Milles', but I didn't like it. Aunt Anna had her group (distinguished guests), Agnes and Margaret had the young men, and Uncle William had his study, to which he and Father frequently withdrew. Uncle William once expressed to Mother a wish that he could have a long and plumy tail to drape across one arm, for making entrances. I would have liked one, too, to make an entrance at the William de Mille house and have someone notice me.

At the Cecil de Milles', there was never any sense of being brushed aside, and no stern formality, although there was a butler. At their dinner table I learned to turn my wineglass

Parties I

down, because I was too young yet to be served (at least Frederick, the butler, had set me out a glass!), and to like cashews.

We had every Christmas dinner there, bringing presents to put under the big tree—the first one, for us, trimmed not with real candles but electric lights—and we took presents away. Uncle Cecil's presents could be fascinating. One year he gave me a small pearl pin, which I liked even better than the sapphire ones he gave his nieces. So, I think, did they.

Presents, though—and even Christmas—were a small, if gleaming part, of the enjoyment there. Any dinner was fun, with Uncle Cecil storytelling and Aunt Constance being kind. Any evening, where we talked around the snores of Sloppy, the English bull, by the living room fire, was a merry time. Often we played games, word games such as "I Packed My Grandmother's Trunk" or "My Minister's Cat." Both required lots of memory and lots of words. Uncle Cecil and Mother might end in a spirited Dead Heat by the time the game arrived at *My minister's cat is a cozy, cute, cuddly, curfewed, clever, coruscating, criminal, corroborating, cautious, carbon, catnip, clean, clerestory, Catholic, colorful, combining, coronary, casual, colloquial, contrary, candy-loving, cheerful, conniptious—cat*. One repetition, one omission, you were out. By then the rest of us were out.

Though I wouldn't have admitted it then, I was sorry when we graduated into poker from that over-qualified cat.

Of course there *were* parties in our Hollywood, too.

My first one was an afternoon with a lot of other six-year-olds at Ruth Lasky (Goldwyn's) grandmother's. Small but formidable, widely known as Mother Lasky, Ruth's grandmother had propelled her son Jesse to the headship of a studio—and her daughter Blanche, Ruth's mother, the most reticent of women, into playing the cornet, during the hard times of her youth, in vaudeville! Mother Lasky could take any children's party in her stride.

Ruth and I were not particularly friends, but at our age

guest lists were arranged by adults, much like marriages of state. If you were invited somewhere, you went, usually gift in hand, and hoped to win a prize to compensate. So I went to Ruth's. I didn't win a prize and, after a decent interval of games and food, I was ready to leave. Mrs. Main, the stand-in chauffeur, had already parked outside. There was barely time for me to hurry home and take a bath (all that cake frosting) before being Mother's escort to the opera. *Good-bye—thank you very much—opera*, I explained to Mother Lasky.

She could hardly believe her ears. There were still peppermints to be eaten, snappercrackers to be cracked. What child in his right mind wouldn't rather stay there than go to an opera? I, as it happened. Next to ballet, I admired opera. Mother, whose musical taste echoed her dramatic one, picked the most athletic operas with the most thumping tunes. Not for her *La Bohème* or *Der Rosenkavalier*—too delicate, too mawkish. She preferred the least mystical of Wagner, the most vigorous of Verdi. Afterwards she would have glorious nightmares while I slept like a top.

Mother Lasky, full of pity for so over-privileged a child, demanded that I telephone home and point out to Mother that the party was still going on. As I couldn't refuse, I made my first attempt at double-talk. Fortunately Mother heard the undertone and, accepting a tyrant's role, cooperated by insisting that I leave. While no doubt Mother Lasky shook her head over my plight, and Ruth finished off the lemonade, I was drinking in *Il Trovatore*, on the edge of my seat. It was a splendid opera to make you forget that though you really felt too old for "Pinning on the Donkey's Tail," you were still no good at it.

Mother Lasky and I never became close. I did better with Ruth. When we were roughing it at the same camp in the Sierras at the ages of fourteen and thirteen, she sent home a snapshot of me inscribed (grudgingly? with surprise? dubiously?) "I am beginning to like her." But it *had* taken a while.

Parties I

Parties were improved, I thought, by dressing up. My first costume party also was a Lasky affair, this time at Uncle Jesse's and Aunt Bessie's. World War I was in full swing; sometimes I caught sight of Auntie Bessie on the Boulevard, exquisite in a Red Cross volunteer's blue veil; this party had a patriotic theme. We attended done up as minute nurses and soldiers or sailors, sizes five and six.

I could never get enough of costume parties. Mother must have become sick of them. While some of the other children borrowed from a studio wardrobe, I never did. (I think there was a corollary to Not Borrowing Unless You Asked, which went: Not Asking a Favor That Can't Be Refused.) Mrs. Borrodaile made up my exotic clothes from my own designs, till I had quite a string of once-used harem pants and medieval skirts. With one exception, I never wore a costume twice.

The Bucklands gave a bang-up costume party when I was eleven, in their handsome living room. I went as a princess, having just been one in a school play. I didn't mind putting on the same crown for a second round. There were several musketeers; Douglas Fairbanks, Sr., had just made *The Three Musketeers*. His blonde niece, however, came as a black-haired gypsy maid —no Milady de Winter, she.

The sensation of the evening, though, was Uncle Wilfred Buckland himself, done up as a hobo so effectively we thought for a while he was a roughneck who had wandered in. Make-up was one of the In opportunities for us, though not so much for me. Mother had recognized, early in her contact with the theatre, that cold cream was useful to the skin, and powder went along with it, but her interest stopped there. If I wanted more, as far as she was concerned, there were lipstick and burnt cork.

I could at least provide a good excuse to my friends for further making-up. I issued invitations to a pirate party, when I got to the eighth grade. Pirates had been on my mind for quite a while. In 1917, when we walked the beach at Balboa where Uncle Cecil made part of *The Woman God Forgot*, I had

131

found sand dollars and tried to believe they were pirate wealth. Mother deplored the fact that I read *Treasure Island* many times and turned away from *David Copperfield*.

I had our basement as a pirate cave, for Joe Kamemura had had one baby more than could be stowed, even in Bibi's elastic bungalow, and moved. The basement was the Caribbean, too. On arrival, every guest—they all were girls—was hustled down the basement steps and made to walk the plank. I had spread cushions underneath the plank (a row of chairs) so no necks would get broken by the plunge to the Deep Six. Cecilia helped me, as Consulting Buccaneer.

We had no casualties until we sat down to eat. There was a topsy-turvy menu written to sound as if dessert came first (soup with croutons was called petit-fours with sauce), but, in fact, dessert, as usual, was last, an ice-cream galleon cleaving through spun-sugar seas. The sugar prickles looked less like billows than a bird's nest, but they were delicious to eat—if you could.

The problem was that several pirates had arrived not only with wigs, but with moustaches and full beards. Those who were able took their moustaches off. My classmate Adele Farnum had been trimmed with whiskers of professional crepe hair by her father, stage and screen star William Farnum. The worst excesses of the Spanish Main hardly exceeded Adele's torment with that spun sugar in the hair.

The climax to the revelries in the eighth grade was a Slumber Party, the idea being that you went to someone's house and tried not to slumber. The hostess was another classmate, Juanita Doubleday, whose parents had come from ranching sheep in Idaho to start a movie company, Two Suns. Their house, too, was close to school, and they were generous in lending the upstairs ballroom, which included a small stage. We took classes in eurythmics there, which hadn't wholly vanished with Miss Press, and gave short and arty plays.

For the Slumber Party, Juanita invited our whole class of

Parties I

twelve to spend the night. We stayed up as long as we could. Still, after dancing and charades and fudge, we giggled into bed by one o'clock. A few stout-hearted souls went on giggling and about an hour later surged back to the ballroom with a frightful din. They intended to make the rest of us angry or ashamed, but, anyway, to get us up. They made someone angry—it was never clear whom—for presently they found themselves locked in. They began to shout and stamp. We slugabeds, who had no idea they were trapped, piled the pillows on our ears.

In another hour, truly pitiful moans got the prisoners freed. By then they were somewhat blue with cold—the California coastal night in May not being suitable for robeless nightgowns and bare feet—and slighty blue with terror, too. The Doubledays kept curios in their ballroom, and, amusing or just queer as these might seem during the day, at night—even with electric lights—the stuffed dog which had been their pet, the pickled tapeworm (nobody's pet, surely), and the strip of human skin (taken from the corpse of a mad woman, it had been explained—or did that really explain?) were, to say the least, disquieting.

The victims were thawed out by morning, and the last coolness melted over hot cakes. We had all put on lounging pajamas, which were the latest fad, and how could you admire another girl's pajamas and have her admire yours, if you didn't speak? Far more admirable, though we never guessed it then, was the courage of the Doubledays in offering such hospitality, for though the party ended well, their company did not. Two Suns was already setting fast, and when most of us appeared as H.S.G. freshmen in the fall, Juanita was already back in Idaho. We had no thought of fall that May, except to believe that when we got to high school, the real, grown-up parties would begin!

XXII
Background Music

During all this time, Mother had been busily writing away for such stars as Wallie Reid, Conrad Nagel, Jack Holt, Ethel Clayton, who had that "fine and gentle sex appeal," Agnes Ayres, and Katherine MacDonald, publicized as "The American Beauty," to whom a director allegedly once said, "Not that expression, dear—the other one, the nauseated one." Mother's favorite actress, though remained Lila Lee, who, as a leading woman not yet turned sixteen, bravely dove into the freezing waters of Big Bear Lake for *The Heart of Youth*.

Novelist Kathleen Norris came to tea. Poet Witter Bynner and playwright Edward Knoblock (then spending a summer in director William Desmond Taylor's bungalow while Taylor had the Knoblock house in England) came to dinner.

Did Mother never wish she were back writing for the stage? She had gloated to her mother, soon after we came West, that at least with the screen there were no First Nights. This was not exactly true. With the specials, there were openings, and with most pictures there were sneak previews meant for getting honest audience reaction, not the half-sneak kind the theatres advertised later just to boost attendance. Mornings after previews could be as dreary as the mornings after First Nights, if you cared about what you were doing. Mother never could learn not to care.

Still, apart from a skit for that twenty-fifth reunion of her

Beulah Marie Dix Flebbe. My mother circa 1922, with her Serious Author's look and a hat my father called a casserole.

Beulah and George Flebbe at home, 1910. Christened Georg Hermann Heinrich Karl Ludwig, Father abridged himself when he applied for U.S. citizenship.

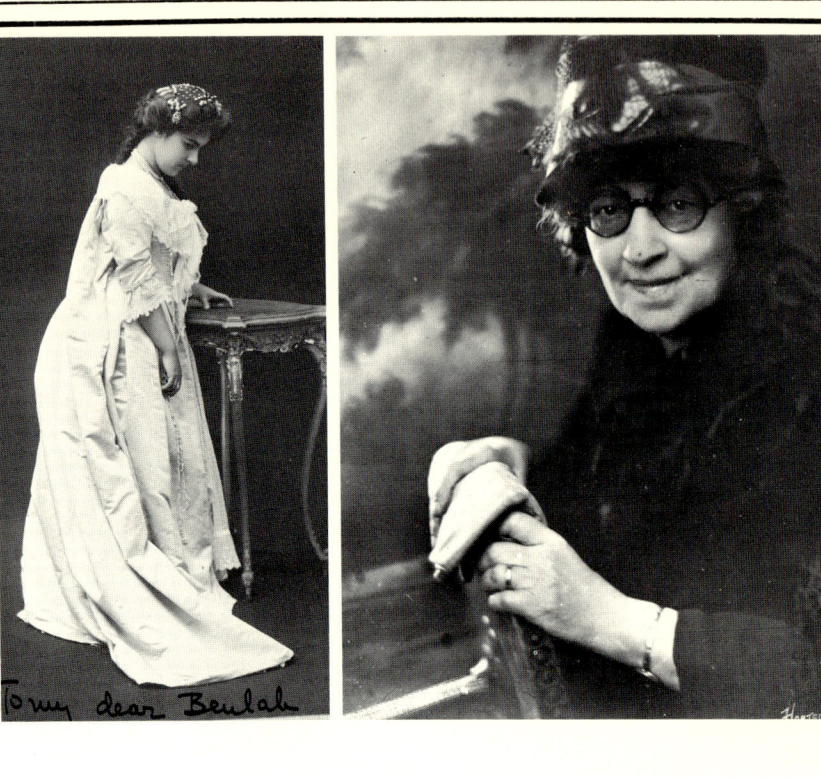

(Above left) Josephine (Sherwood) Hull, a fellow-graduate of Mother's in the Radcliffe class of '97. (At right) Bibi. Mrs. Henry de Mille, mother of "the boys" William and Cecil, as she looked when we arrived in Hollywood.

(Top) Patriotic party, 1917. Host Jesse Lasky, Jr., sits at left, his mother at right in front of Jesse, Sr. Ruth Lasky, Billy Buckland, four de Milles and I, between. (Bottom) Buckland party, 1922. Katherine de Mille in Dutch cap; Noah Beery, Jr., in chaps; hobo Wilfred Buckland on stairs.

The Call of the East on location at Big Bear Lake, 1917. Far left, future director James Cruze, then an actor; Mother; Sessue Hayakawa, watching his wife. Jack Holt, center rear.

(Top) *Nan of Music Mountain*, Big Bear, 1917, Front, third from left, Margaret Loomis. Seated, from right, director George Melford, Ann Little, Wallace Reid, Dorothy Davenport Reid. Wrangler Jack Hoxie stands hatless. (Bottom) Father and pilot Thompson, Mexico, 1922.

(Top) Father between Mercury pilots. Cars are Roamers, one of them ours; the photograph was used as a Roamer ad. (Bottom) David Thompson with his plane after the air accident during *The Grim Game*.

The Ostrich Farm and the Alligator Farm were our Disneylands in 1918. Father had just learned that ostriches kick.

(Top left) Mother and I, dressed for outdoor set-watching; photo taken by Harry Houdini. (Center) Angel of Mercy, Argyle Avenue. (Top right) Cecilia de Mille, age eight, in *Carmen* clothes. (Below) The Balboa Palisades Anti-Sunburn Club—Bibi, Mother, and I.

Joe and Mary Kamemura with their first baby.

(Top) The Montessori class at the Hollywood School for Girls. Juanita Doubleday, center, with curls; Tom Comfort down right; myself in scowling heap. (Bottom) School production of *The Forest Ring*. Left, Irene Mayer, Agnes de Mille, Ben Alexander kneeling.

(Top left) Drama Club. Future designer Natalie Visart and future actress Mary Mason in front. (Top right) Jean Harlow, 1926. (Below) Her classmates. Virginia Parsons, left; Isabelle Belknap fifth from left; third from right, Mary Anita Loos.

(Top left) Margaret de Mille. (Top right) Agnes de Mille. (Bottom left) Olive Borden, who left the screen to be an evangelist. (Bottom right) Janet Riesenfeld. In Spain to study dance, she witnessed the first five months of the Civil War.

(Top) Production sketch for *Creation*, which was never filmed. The animal models turned up in *King Kong*. (Bottom) *The Road to Yesterday*, 1925. Sally Rand is brandishing the mug.

(Top) Geraldine Farrar at the stake in *Joan the Woman*, 1916. (Bottom) *The Road to Yesterday*—Joseph Schildkraut as a proud lord with Jetta Goudal as an even prouder gypsy, also doomed to die at the stake.

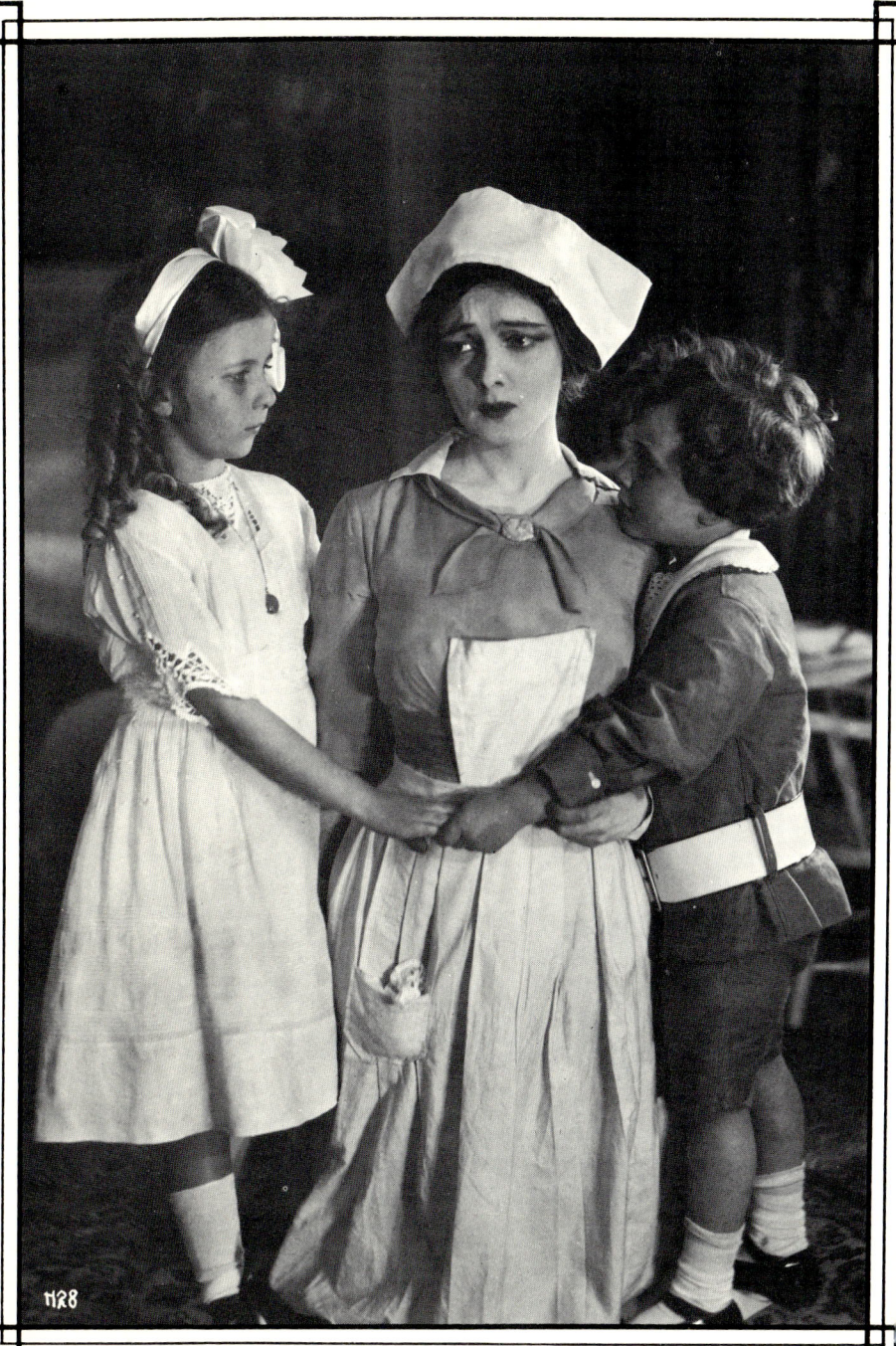

Marie Doro (center) with Margaret de Mille (billed as Peggy George) and Billy Jacobs in *The Heart of Nora Flynn*, 1916. Cecil de Mille directed; Hector Turnbull wrote the screenplay.

Background Music

college class, she wasn't writing plays. This left the field to me, and I established my claim with a one-act melodrama for my French class. It was called *The Sweetness of the Bitter* in the great tradition of *The Cost of Hatred*, but our teacher, who translated it (how could we have acted it in French otherwise?), took a coward's way and retitled it *La Duchesse Anne*.

I was better publicized for this script, which took two nights of scribbling after school, than Mother for the writings of eight years. Evidently there was a coincidental dearth of subjects for the rotogravure section of the *Los Angeles Times*. *La Duchesse Anne* took up a whole page, with the cast looking terribly innocent, medieval, and intent. The caption referred to "the original French play by Evelyn Flebbe, Age 11," and the school roof fell in on me. All my best friends knew I had not set down a single word in French and some of them refused to believe I never had pretended to.

Our teacher gave a shrug—not Gallic; she was Swiss. Would it have been newsworthy had she emphasized that *she* did the translating? she asked. Mother could have learned a few things about promotion from her. Quietly, instead, she plugged away on pictures for Uncle Cecil, on a Western and on *The Spanish Dancer* for Pola Negri, who had been imported from Germany to be Gloria Swanson's only real rival as a *femme fatale*. Then Mother gave her heart to her original, *Borderland*. I refused to see it, for, at the end, a brave dog died trying to rescue an abandoned child from a burning house. Mother cried just telling me about it. But she wasn't *unhappily* sad. She still felt that she was doing mostly good work, that she would do better, and that even if not growing famous, she was nicely paid. It may not have been quite the time of the singing of birds—which with us would have been mockingbirds—but it had a lilt.

There was also background music.

The movies were silent, of course, but not *quite* as silent. More and more, musical outlines, if not outright scores, were

prepared to go along with films, so the theatre pianist or organist would not endlessly repeat "The Ride of the Valkyrie" for a chase or "The Spring Song" for the change of season. Theme songs were only a few notes ahead, and before long we would be singing "Charmaine" from *The Big Parade* just as eagerly as if it had been recorded on the film.

The nearest music, though, was on the set. Most companies made use of an orchestra, or at least a piano, to put actors in the mood for love scenes after breakfast or death scenes after lunch. On Uncle Cecil's set, the orchestra also piped the principals aboard. If you heard the strains of "Hail to the Chief," you knew the director had arrived. If you heard *"Cielito Lindo,"* that meant Mother was hopping across cables to her chair. Music closer to her character would have been some bars of Stephen Foster mixed with "Lillibullero," but she loved *"Cielito Lindo,"* which she first heard on a record Father brought from Mexico.

"The happy summer of 1920" she had labeled the months following the Montessori year. 1921 and 1922 were not bad either, even without location, even with censorship.

But there came another dissonance.

Hardly had the movies grown evil and rich when the outside world was clamoring to share the evil gain. People leaped up from Washington to Florida to claim their ideas had been seized to star that winsome ingenue, that leering villain, even that appealing horse or dog. "Why, that was what I thought up, for the boy and girl to get acquainted at the hashery!" "Why, I wrote in to say they should make a movie from *Lord Fauntleroy!*" the cries rose above the crash of piano chords at the finale of a film. "Pirate" was added to the other bad names being shied at movie people—and no victim of such piracy meant to be paid in sand dollars.

Many of the claimants did act in good faith. They really thought that they had rights to a fundamental plot or deserved a finder's fee for pointing to a classic found on everybody's

Background Music

shelves. The movies weren't *that* rich. Judge and jury didn't seem so sure. While plagiarism still was being defined, in a movie sense, there was a tendency for courts to favor the poor fellow with a sick wife and six kids who said he had invented Boy Meets Girl. What could a few thousand dollars more mean to Paramount? A great deal, when you considered that the claimant could claim damages in every separate state where a film was shown. He was almost sure to win in his home state, for a start, which would set a precedent.

It became essential for the movies to have legal precedents that would protect the use of general ideas, or the Bible would be the only source movie makers dared use.

The Bible, though, was the subject of the first suit on which Mother worked. Twice she was a witness and an expert for Uncle Cecil, the first time on his first *Ten Commandments*. This *Ten Commandments*, like *Joan the Woman*, had a modern story along with the ancient one, but the suit concerned the ancient part!

In her deposition, Mother quoted passage after passage of the Old Testament ("The thing which I greatly feared is come upon me ... deep calleth unto deep ... Arise, shine ..."), not only to demonstrate her knowledge of the subject, but to make the point that movie writers were not necessarily irreligious or illiterate. Then she cited prior literary use of Old Testament material to show the historic pattern of reversion to this source. The facts, and the way she marshaled them, so impressed the plaintiff's attorney that he told her she should have been a lawyer. Lawyers usually did.

The second legal bout was over a screenplay which was partly hers, *Feet of Clay*. It had a sequence on the astral plane. The main characters, after rakish deeds such as aquaplaning around Catalina Island (this caused heroine Vera Reynolds to dive into cold water, too,) catapulted into limbo, towards an awesome judgment of souls. Sutton Vane, author of the recently successful play *Outward Bound*, which took place in

limbo, shouted infringement. Mother rolled back her sleeves to prove that just as no one can fence in the Bible, so no one can stake out a claim to the astral plane.

She was somewhat annoyed by Sutton Vane. Eight years before, her *Across the Border* had a scene in limbo. When *Outward Bound* opened in New York, she hadn't sued Sutton Vane, had she?

Uncle Cecil won both suits, and the quantity of suits fell off as legal guidelines were set—there had to be a *sequence* of similar events, not just one, to support a case—and it grew clear that studios weren't sitting ducks. Mother saved a few anecdotes to swap with Zach Cobb, that El Paso Customs Collector, now a lawyer in Los Angeles. He confided to her that during the border troubles back in 1915–1916, he had wired President Wilson at a tense moment, "This cheapening of American life must stop." What a subtitle! Mother thought.

She wasn't writing plays, but she wrote a book, her first since *Hands Off!* in 1919, and this one, published in 1922, was a juvenile. Much of it took place on a farm, recognizably my aunt's, with one character much like my aunt, and two youthful heroines disturbingly, if not revoltingly, like me. What I disliked most was that one of them kept muttering strange oaths ("Shivering chimpanzees!"), which for a short time I had done. But that was *last* year, when I was ten. Mother wondered if I could be jealous (her rival—with my *Duchess Anne?*) when I had to be excused for "a glass of water" while she was reading us the galleys. I was just ashamed.

Bibi was a better critic and she liked the book. She had quit writing, she had finished decorating, but she always had a dozen projects and a hundred interests. Her eyes danced one day when she brought an armful of new dresses home. She had charged them to Uncle Cecil. "He buys other women clothes," she remarked to Mother. "Why not me?" Not long after this she bought a diamond.

I had been told that Uncle Cecil jingled uncut jewels in his

Background Music

pocket the way Father jingled change. I had never seen them, though, and my first look at loose precious stones was to watch them shaken out in front of Bibi on our dining table. The jeweler dropped them from black tissue paper, and they flashed a hundred tones. Bibi picked one that was faintly green, which I, too, preferred to the merely white or blue. She ordered it mounted, not in old-fashioned gold or new-fashioned platinum, but in a miniature black box to be worn with a black cord. I thought such *un*ostentation was the summit of magnificance.

But in spite of the new clothes and the new diamond, Bibi began spending quiet week ends at the beach. She rented an apartment at Long Beach; the address was to be kept a secret, even from her relatives, to ensure entire rest. Mother went along. Maybe the apartment mainly was for Mother—having moonlighted a book, she was slightly quenched.

Some week ends I, too, visited "The Perch." The adults could remain quiet even if I was there, for I would be out on the beach and the beach was widely known as safe. In a way, it was. The bottom of the sea was flat, up and down and out, for miles. Still, it was the only beach where I cut my foot in the same place twice. Both the same place on the foot and the same place on the beach.

Otherwise, the secrecy about our address was the one excitement to The Perch, and the drive to Long Beach I thought hideous. You had to go right through industrial Los Angeles (the first freeway wasn't until 1936, and then it went east, not south) and skirt Watts, a hamlet with some farms. Vaudeville comedians who wanted to make local jokes during a stand at the Orpheum referred to Watts—"Who was that dude from Watts I saw you with last night?"—until they heard of Calabasas, slightly farther off. They did much with the fact that the name Calabasas meant calabash (squash), unaware it was in fact a corruption of the Indian Calahuasa, which identified a vanished Chumash village. Neither could they, nor the Orpheum's best seers and mystics, dream that, one day, burning

and riots would efface any last atmosphere of humor about Watts.

We had hardly recovered from the stimulation of seeing *The Turned About Girls* in print, when Mother sold a book to Richard Barthelmess, the ex-Griffith star who now headed his own company. It was *The Fighting Blade*, the one whose hero was my father in a baldric and jack boots. This meant extra cash and an extra impetus to go to Europe. Mother had been thinking for some time that I ought to be exposed to Rembrandts, castles, landscapes, and my grandparents. Life in California could give a limited, if sunny, view. Now we would stretch my sphere.

We couldn't stretch it until well into June of 1923, because You Don't Take the Children out of School. On this occasion I concurred with the Commandment. I was about to graduate from the eighth grade, a moment of importance then. There was quite a good deal doing, in June, for all the grades. At the close of my first term at H.S.G., I had been asked to sing. The number was "Under the Apple Tree." As I finished, nervously, I smirked. All the other children's parents laughed. Mother thought me rude; Father said it looked as though I had a tic. I never undertook a solo publicly again. Did they ever sense an opportunity missed when Helen Kane (the Boop-boop-a-doop Girl) made a whole career from getting through a lyric too soon and filling out the beat with Boop-boop-a-doop? What was wrong with a career of smirks?

After that I tried not to be noticed at graduations. The worst that happened now, in the eighth grade, was that, following our hike from the recesses of the grounds, singing "Ancient of Days" (also off the beat because the piano, till you got to the assembly on the lawn, seemed half a mile away), the pianist asked me to turn her pages. I instantly lost touch with any trace of sight reading and turned too soon.

Bibi came to the graduation ceremony, bringing me a silver filigree cardcase with my monogram and the calling cards as

Background Music

well. Never again was I to feel so meaningful. She declined to come to Europe with us, though. She was too engaged, with her garden, the birds, The Perch. . . .

The day after my graduation, we leaped on the train and then on the ship and our sphere stretched. In a way it shrank, too, for when we got back to Argyle Avenue, Bibi wasn't there. She had died before we even knew that she was ill. She hadn't wished to worry us or cut short our trip.

We missed her very much, the way her Packard roadster with the batik curtains jounced up our drive, the way she looked across her glasses, or looked for them, and the way she smiled. The things she said, the things she didn't say—the beads, the combs, the veils, the person who shot sparks behind the veils.

Cielito Lindo, the lovely sky, never would be quite so blue.

XXIII
Famous Girl

A lot of things were different.

When we got back from Europe, hemlines were down, overnight. My three Paris dresses (not originals, but nice) looked like Russian blouses, ending as they did at the knees. In school, where we had now adopted uniforms of middy and skirt, we wore serge to the instep.

Still, at H.S.G. had anything else truly changed? The school motto was *Labore ac veritate*—something, Mother said, about achieving truth through work. Arithmetic we now called math. History was government. We would have Chemistry in place of nature talks. Basically, the work for truth seemed the same.

We looked back into the grades (otherwise you looked into the pine) and found them still composed of the usual neighborhood-and-movie blend. Back there almost at the bottom was Rosemary Conway, with blue eyes that could reach right across the school. Her father, Jack Conway, had been a Griffith leading man before he began directing, too. Her seatmate was a girl from the duplex opposite the school. Then came Marjorie Bell whose father, curiously named Monta, both directed and wrote. Behind them was Dorothy Sills whose father, Milton, was so sinewy and staunch as *The Sea Hawk*, a great hit of 1924. A pair of small girls, Evelyn and Marion Edwards, were not only daughters of Snitz Edwards, the comedian prominent in Fair-

banks pictures and once proudly known as the ugliest actor in New York, but they lived in the neighborhood and had a pony cart. Horses were thinning out in central Hollywood—a single surrey with a fringe sometimes ventured near our house—but a pony cart was safe on the side roads near the school.

Looking forward, Agnes de Mille and Cecilia's and Katie's half-aunt Nancy had got out of high school by the fall when I got in. Irene Mayer, the tarantella, was well on her way. That year the school publication summarized her, "Wisdom and wit; but better than these is pep." This was a motto we all understood. Sex appeal had begun to be Subject A with us, but we suspected you got born with it. You could practice pep.

I practiced so well that one study hour I burst out of the barn on an impulse without asking permission of the monitor. I was hauled before the student-government board. Cecilia was its head. "Look before you leap," was her Solomon-like comment. "He who hesitates is lost," I pepped back, and got two demerits, one for breaking classroom rules and one for being flippant with the government.

One of my new classmates was a part-time actress. Earlier I had been blasé about acting claims. (Didn't everybody say they acted? Hadn't everybody, even I?) But after discovering that a fellow sixth grader, whom I thought (for some reason probably connected with our incompatibility) never had been near the screen, was in fact featured as an infant player in *The Squaw Man*, I grew more tolerant. So now I accepted that Dolores, a tomboy and thirteen, had to keep her sausage curls in case she got called on for a part. Right beside her, also in curls and, to my mind, more significant, was a girl whose father had designed those Pig'n Whistle pigs.

The biggest tomboy in school (surprisingly, we thought) was Frances Rich. Her mother, Irene, was our screen ideal of sophistication and high style. Actually, Irene Rich had been a leading woman for folksy Will Rogers, rough-hewn Harry Carey, and Strongheart, the famous dog, before she became a

star. Frances, just as versatile, was to serve as naval lieutenant during World War II, and become a sculptor.

At the back of our barn, Betty Lee, from the Deep South, was so homesick that she never studied but played solitaire and whistled "Dixie" under her breath. At the front sat the prettiest girl in school, Lillian, who had brown velvet eyes, lashes almost like ball fringe, red hair she could sit on, and a rosebud skin. She came from a theatrical background and there seemed no question but that she would act.

One morning when we were sitting in the chemistry shed—Lillian on her long hair—our science teacher, Mr. Lucas, told us he meant to try an experiment which might possibly blow up. Mr. Lucas was a good-looking young man not entirely protected from a certain ardor in his pupils by the fact that he had a wife. He told lively tales about his past, when he had been an undertaker's helper, and occasionally he acted in one of Uncle Cecil's films. He was, in fact, a bit theatric. He got a performance out of Lillian.

She said if the experiment was likely to blow up, she would have to be allowed to leave. She could not, professionally, risk scarring her face. This did not to me seem Playing the Game. (I was still a year or two from the revelation at the beach, through Margaret de Mille, that sometimes you weren't playing at all.) Mr. Lucas hastily explained it was a joke.

Then there was the girl in the class just after mine.

My father, who liked simple jokes, too, used to call us the Hollywood School for Squirrels. She surely has remained our most celebrated squirrel. Her name was Harlean Carpenter.

Harlean entered H.S.G. when I was twelve, that first year we wore uniforms. The uniform never looked on anybody else the way it looked on her. Other girls broke the rule against pinning in your middy blouse tight at the waist—only on Harlean did this really overcome the package-y effect. Father's real estate office was just a few blocks from school, opposite the Hollywood Hotel. After school, the girls would wander by.

Famous Girl

They all just walked, he said, except Harlean—she sashayed.

It would have been nice to be her friend. I think I would have liked to but I couldn't find out how. Girls with a purpose fascinated and alarmed me. At thirteen, her eyes did not reflect the wisdom of the ages, but they did look somewhere, which was more than mine did.

I went "over to Harlean's" one day after school. She lived with her mother in a minor Sunset Boulevard mansion which was then a rooming house. I had been in mansions but not rooming houses. Were there special ways to behave—less noise, less dust on your feet? Harlean's mother bothered me, too. She was blonde and vivacious in a way that mothers of my closer friends were not.

Harlean was excessively blonde. She had the first young white hair I or any one around had ever seen. There were two opinions on its color, or non-color. One was that it was a genuine gift from the elves who hovered round her crib. The other, founded on the report of a classmate who knew her well, was that Mrs. Carpenter began to bleach her daughter's hair soon after birth. Natural or not, Harlean created a type, and if her skin was not the fragile white usually seen in the ultra-fair, that just made her more unique. There she sat at her desk—smoldering like tow.

In her second year at H.S.G. we grew no chummier. I was a recruiter—Woodcraft, basketball, the French club, the yearbook. With a school as small as ours, you had to be, or activities did not survive. Harlean was no easy recruit. The only activity she cared about was Expression, as we called our drama class, and our teacher said she showed no promise at all; even in a school as small as ours there was indecision as to whether she could be admitted to the drama club.

After she was admitted, something beyond H.S.G. still seemed on her mind, of which I got an inkling late one afternoon.

I was pawing round for my bookbag in the cloakroom off

the study hall, and stabbing a finger with a splinter as I did, when I heard her talking with her best friend, Marge. I glanced into the study hall. Everybody else had left. Harlean sat at her desk, chin in hand, white hair tilted to one side, listening to Marge wind up what must have been a long harangue: "The average young millionaire of nineteen or twenty isn't going to throw himself and his fortune at your feet."

I don't know what Harlean answered, if she did.

Very shortly after that, she married a millionaire. If he wasn't quite, he was close enough. She was with him on the Beach Club veranda once when I was playing volleyball out on the sand. Her hair was pure platinum against a black cartwheel hat. I supposed she had got where she wanted.

She had just begun.

The next time I saw her was at Fox, the "old" Fox Studio in Hollywood, at Sunset Boulevard and Western Avenue. The new one at Fox Hills, next door to Beverly Hills, was just being built. The property, in fact, which would soon be the main Twentieth-Century-Fox plant (and far later the highrise mall-and-fountain Century City), was as yet so wild and untamed that Mother's picture *Black Magic*, a fine version of "the natives are restless tonight" plot, went out on location there.

That day at the old Fox, Harlean was in grease paint and was hurrying to work—extra work, I presumed. While some of my best friends (and of everyone's, in Hollywood) sometimes worked as extras, this was not the glowing way to go. A setback for Harlean?

Definitely not. Very soon afterwards she was Jean Harlow, in *Hell's Angels*, and a star. She was in electric lights, and electric on the screen, though she had a stilted part. As usual, we went to the premiere.

Premieres were by then the ultimate display for Hollywood. First only the Egyptian Theatre, with its Arab sentry on guard on the roof, had had them. Then so did the Chinese and

Famous Girl

still other theatres. There were always trimmings of crowds, police, loudspeakers, lights blazing on the Rollses, Cadillacs, and Packards, and on us in the de Mille Mercedes, inching up the Boulevard, while strangers pressed their faces to the glass to see if we were "someone" and then fell back complaining we were no one after all. It would make you feel for a moment that your satin and chiffon—perhaps an orchid or two—had been blotted off the earth.

Still, going to premieres, you asked for it. You got out of your car behind Ronald Colman, Richard Arlen, or Rod LaRocque, and you tried to hurry down the red carpet politely, for behind the ropes the public strained to see Constance Bennett, Pola Negri, or Joan Crawford, who were in your wake. Mother hated openings but she knew she had to go. The new picture was all Hollywood discussed, next day. *Hell's Angels* was an especially exciting opening for me, not because of Harlean.

The next morning, at the beach, that other schoolmate Joel McCrea told me I had looked well the night before. He rubbed my back as I lay sleepily in my backless bathing suit and all but purred on the delightfully hot sand under the (suddenly) delightfully scorching sun.

Success was slightly different for Harlean. She got married two times more, and some critics came to the decision that she really *could* act. There was inevitably lots of talk about her, that she had no talent and no figure, that she simply used a lot of tricks—like not wearing a brassiere! We were still unpeeling from an era when a girl went round bound above the waist like a papoose.

Years afterwards a neighbor assured me that, back then, her husband telephoned her after a domestic quarrel to taunt her that he was in bed with Jean. If this was true (dubious), how much nicer for your husband to be unfaithful to you with the Blonde Bombshell than with Zoë Doe.

You could hear anything. The worst thing we squirrels

from H.S.G. ever *knew* about Harlean was her true name. We loved to salute her with "Hello, Harlean." It gave a sense of inside information, I suppose, and perhaps of bringing someone down. It was small of us, but we were very young. She was not so small. She would answer courteously.

The last time I saw her was in the Ladies' Room of a Valley club. We attended the same party. It was no momentous encounter. We were just acquaintances. The conversation ran to "Gorgeous earrings"—"gorgeous dress."

Then she died, so she stayed young, and can be seen without any blurring by age of that sultry face and sashaying figure—without any dimming of that blinding hair.

XXIV
Under the Pickle Sign

We had always said we lived in Hollywood where movies were made. To suggest that quite a few of them got made in the San Fernando Valley or in Culver City was a quibble. Now we quibbled. Uncle Cecil went to Culver City. He took over the old Ince premises, round the bend from Metro-Goldwyn-Mayer, and set up a studio entirely his own. We hurried for a look.

Culver City was a small, though not bucolic, town, surrounded by fields which were either bare or done in vegetables by Japanese and Japanese-Americans. Back of the four business blocks and a three-sided hotel ran Ballona Wash, a real Western draw, dry as cowhide most of the year and a torrent for a day or two. Back of that rose the Baldwin Hills with their oil rig battlements.

One flank of the hills was branded with a giant "57," advertising Heinz products in their infinite variety. At summer camp Katie de Mille and I met a girl who lived a ranch life underneath the "57." It made a bond for me with those fields and hills. I'm not sure Mother ever had one.

I assumed that she left Paramount to follow Uncle Cecil by her own free choice, until one day she remarked that our European trip divorced her from her job. Every year her Paramount contract had been renewed, with a raise. The next fall it was not. She could make a brilliant analysis of the intrigues of Queen Elizabeth the First; but she would take no

part in intrigue. I don't think she had real enemies; but her solid figure and her solid convictions when it came to story-points may have sometimes got in people's way. So did her vocabulary, but she felt it impolite to "talk down."

I think Paramount money men, who never understood and in some ways feared her, took for granted she was part of the de Mille group, and would not be happy or productive left behind. Perhaps she wanted to be asked. Perhaps she simply hated giving up the black and white and orange cretonne.

The style was different, at the new studio—those colors wouldn't do. Uncle Cecil's emblem, an armed knight on a charging steed, swung above luxurious green lawn. (The gardener, it was said, was a descendant of Pio Pico, California's first governor.) Behind the lawn and a half-moon drive stood the offices—a white plantation house. Since there was a roadhouse called The Plantation just a few miles west, pleasure seekers sometimes met with bitter disappointment turning up the drive of De Mille Productions after dark and finding the great ivory doors that seemed to promise julep and fried chicken closed and locked.

Mother had her office on the second floor. All directors and writers were on that floor except Uncle Cecil, who had a suite on the third floor, with a white bearskin rug. The reading and research department was up there, too, run by Aunt Constance's stepmother. Nepotism in the industry had always been widespread; working relatives of studio executives were of two kinds—hopeless, sometimes brazen, misfits, and capable, devoted employees trying twice as hard against the odds of both familiarity and some contempt. Aunt Constance's stepmother belonged to the second kind.

Culver City got us into transportation problems. Portal to portal, Mother had to cover some ten miles. She could no longer walk home, if my father wasn't round with the car, so at last she learned to drive, but barely. She and Father made the classic mistake of his teaching her. He was manually dextrous;

Under the Pickle Sign

she was physically addled. As to her splendid mind, though part of it was wracked all day with forebodings of the intersections she must cross on the way home, when she really got behind the wheel, she would think about a script.

She did *try*, in her own armor of a rigid spine and leather gloves, with a blue Chandler for her horse. The Chandler was equipped with balloon tires, very up-to-date, which didn't add to giving her an easy time. On the other hand, she gave *it* no easy time; it also had non-strippable gears—she stripped them. After that, and a small brush with a bicycle (the bicyclist was shaken—Mother was shattered), we had a chauffeur till I reached fourteen, the legal age to get a driver's license.

I visited the studio-plantation after school almost every day, in the cause of transportation. My middy and skirt seemed a little out of keeping, but this was made up for by the other people in the high white entry or on the long sweep of lobby stairs. I met most of Uncle Cecil's stars on the stairs—Leatrice Joy, who for a while was Mrs. John Gilbert, Rod LaRocque, Bill Boyd, Phyllis Haver. Phyllis was such an enchanting blonde; Mother wholly believed a story that, stopped for speeding by a Culver City policeman who sternly asked her name, she replied, "Phyllis, what's yours?" with such a lovely smile that she went free.

There were also handsome, dashing young women used to light up the background of a film, with the hope that some day one of them might flame up in a Roman candle of ability. One was a tall, beautiful redhead. One was a tall, beautiful brunette. One was a small brunette with such a lush figure that the vulgar comment in the halls was if she ran up those long stairs, she would black her eyes. (Hearing little vulgarity, I thought this was wit.)

She had sparkling—sizzling—eyes, but not through them did she grow famous. In Chicago at the World's Fair she picked up a few fans (feather) and a horde of fans (human) to become the world's most celebrated fan dancer, Sally Rand.

No De Mille Studio star turned into another Gloria Swanson or another Wallie Reid. Mother's theory—unlike common belief—was that Uncle Cecil was no star maker. Swanson, it was true, had stepped from comedies to drama and esteem through him, but her talent was a natural force, similar to Garbo's, and you could hardly imagine her *not* being a success. No one else who started small with him grew to such height, unless you could count Bill Boyd, a minor hero for de Mille, a major one as the great, early television idol Hoppy.

It hardly mattered. Uncle Cecil was the real star of whatever he produced. A twist of the most recent style, a dash of the risqué, a dollop of the violent, a splash of costume—perhaps a bit of Bible, too—and he served up a feast to thrill the public taste. The feast he prepared not long after reaching Culver City was *The Road to Yesterday*, based on the play Mother wrote with Evelyn Sutherland. The play was about reincarnation.

Mother was for reincarnation. That is not to say she always believed in it; she thought it an intelligent idea. What was the sense of learning how to open cans in this life, always a chore for her, if you couldn't use the character you thus developed in some life beyond? Then there were those half-memories hinting at a distant past and there was the seeming injustice in so many tragedies. After Mrs. Sutherland's death, Mother poured her grief into a melancholy book, where modern beings found out through their dreams how their misfortunes grew from mistakes they had made in other lives.

In *The Road to Yesterday*, modern beings had discovered this through dreams—but it wasn't melancholy, it was filled with swashbuckling and bounce. After bouncing to Broadway in play form, it became an operetta, too, *The Dream Girl*, with a Victor Herbert score. Now it would be a de Mille special, for which Mother wrote the scenes of flash-back dreams, while Jeanie Macpherson updated the modern part.

The crux of the plot was the aversion the heroine developed

for her bridegroom on their wedding night. The heroine was to be Jetta Goudal and the bridegroom Joseph Schildkraut, both fresh from New York. De Mille Studio discovered they had brought along a genuine and mutual aversion, never quite explained.

Jetta had all kinds of mystery. First there were her looks. Nobody else had such a face. She was temple bells, a peacock throne, a painted veil—and she could act. The rumors flew. Was she Indo-Chinese? From Tibet? Dutch? Mata Hari's daughter? Mata Hari in the flesh? (The same sort of curiosity was to surge years later over Audrey Hepburn—was she Indo-Chinese? Mata Hari's granddaughter? Jetta Goudal's daughter?)

It was also bruited that Jetta Goudal had her moments of "temperament," and that Joseph Schildkraut had vowed he would never act with her, or ride a horse. In *The Road to Yesterday* he ended doing both. What was more, each of these attractive players felt the same side of his (her) face photographed the best. Since it is awkward to shoot romantic scenes with both of a pair of lovers always looking to the right, problems grew.

The picture was intensely romantic. Early in the plot, the bridal couple left on their honeymoon, by train. They really did leave—they were going to the Grand Canyon, with the crew, where Uncle Cecil would film Joseph breaking down a door the bride had locked on him in the venerable Harvey House hotel. Bacon and waffles never were like this!

We went to the station to wave the company good-bye, but Mother didn't board the train. She wasn't needed for the sequence, and I think she felt relieved. We had been at the Grand Canyon earlier with Bibi, and had had a lovely time, pointing out rock colors from the lookouts, hiking part way down Bright Angel Trail. It was even fun when Bibi lost her trunk key. With Mother as chief sleuth, we ferreted it out in the toe of a bedroom slipper in an overnight bag, quite a

logical place, as Bibi pointed out, if you didn't need to get into your trunk until you went to bed. We had lived with memories of Bibi, at home, till they were a little blunt, but at the Harvey House they would still be sharp.

So Mother sat upstairs in Culver City smoothing the scenes which explained the ruined honeymoon. Seventeenth-century Joseph, lord of a bankrupt manor and determined on a rich marriage, had abandoned his protesting gypsy sweetheart Jetta to be burned as a witch.

Maybe anticipation of so harrowing a scene set Jetta's nerves on edge. Adrian, the young costume designer whose name would be known at least half as widely as de Mille, collapsed after a fitting with her.

The costumes were superb. Joseph, who had starred in *Liliom* and *The Firebrand* on Broadway, never did look handsomer, though he would win more renown as the seedy, stubborn, unromantic Dreyfus in *The Life of Émile Zola*. In *The Road to Yesterday* he had a costume of black suede, faced with gilded leather, a pearl hanging from one ear. When Cecilia told me he had kissed her hand from palm to elbow so adroitly that she never felt it, I was too impressed to ask her how she knew.

The burning of Jetta was to be at night, on the De Mille Studio back lot, and now I was old enough to stay up and watch. It was cold (*in California, a coat!*), but not for her. A dummy, of course, was standing, or in this case slumping by, for the long shots as the heroine expired—not forgiving, like Joan of Arc, but hurling curses on the villain who betrayed her.

For close-ups, Jetta herself was lashed to the stake, and a fire lit a little distance off so the smoke would blow across her lovely, anguished face. Just as the close-ups ended, the wind shifted, and the smoke and flame blew, not across, but *at* the stake. It was several moments—of acute discomfort for the star—before anybody realized she was still lashed tight.

She made other pictures for De Mille Studio, notably

Under the Pickle Sign

Three Faces East, on which Mother worked. But though she had a lot of passionate admirers, she never did become the ranking favorite her looks and talent justified. She may have been a trifle too exotic or too temperamental. Mother thought she wasn't strong. A decade afterwards, my father and I met her and her husband, a respected decorator, over a tennis net. She not only looked in perfect health but radiant with good humor. She also looked like Mata Hari in a tennis skirt.

Movies in those days still were sold to theatres via block booking, which was later stopped by law because it forced a theatre owner to accept and show pictures he might not want, in order to get those he did. It meant that Uncle Cecil had to make many more pictures at De Mille Studio than he could personally direct—enough to fill a program for a year—or De Mille Studio would not be able to compete.

One day he plainly felt that managing a plant and personnel, as well as shooting his own films and supervising those the other units shot, was more than just one genius could achieve. The plantation doors closed for a longer period than overnight; the armored knight jogged away down that Culver City road.

XXV
Set-watching

We didn't *just* have movies and movie sets to turn to for our entertainment.

Sports, for instance—Vernon, founded southeast of Los Angeles by a nephew of the Calabasas "Baron" Leonis, claimed from 1908 until the 1920s to be boxing capital of the world. I never got there but I did work my way up to attending Friday night prizefights at the Hollywood Legion Stadium, which became a Hollywood must.

With tennis, if we couldn't absolutely believe that California invented it, we did know it had been revised by California players, especially the Sutton sisters, who went to Wimbledon with short dresses and bare heads in 1908 when other women on the courts wore picture hats and tea gowns. For riding, Beverly Hills offered a bridle trail "from the mountains to the sea," down which Hobart Bosworth, Selig's first great star, still cantered his white horse—in the twenties —every day. There were lots of horse shows; we sat with Aunt Constance while Cecilia drove or rode.

Perhaps this wasn't what our Eastern friends might mean by culture? Well, we had museums, even if not quite the Louvre. Mother managed not to know we had a first-rank Indian museum, but we did see a remarkable private collection of *kachinas*, sacred Indian dolls. We had music, though Mother rather left the symphony to Bibi and Aunt Constance. We had real, "legitimate" theatre. Bibi took me to see Sarah Bernhardt

Set-watching

at the Orpheum, between the magic feats and the trick seals. Bernhardt appeared in a sketch as a poilu with one leg—she had lost a leg—to raise money for French war orphans. My impression was of someone leaning on a tree, to a great deal of applause.

Mother took me to see Ethel Barrymore and Duse. We viewed Ethel Barrymore in *Déclassé*—Mother translated the word and some of the theme—and Duse in *Ghosts*, which took a little briefing for me, too. Such performances were worth the drive into the city, and the getting to bed late, but too often "New York companies" bringing us Shakespeare or last season's hits brought us also grubby scenery and feeble supporting casts.

Once, at least, our local little theatre seemed superior.

It was an extended bungalow, only a few blocks from home. On the summer evenings, doors stood open down both sides giving an effect of open air which, alas, did not prevent the Fire Department from condemning the building soon, as minus proper exits. Even with the doors open, little sound of traffic drifted in. There *was* little sound of traffic, circa 1918, after half-past eight.

The special program I remember was made up of one-act plays and the last one was a dance-pantomime. I was spellbound, for I still intended then to dance. (I gave up this career in high school when I found that unless I worked at ballet every day, I would never stop feeling sore, perhaps not even then, and that I would have no time to play tennis, write, paint, or get As. Only Agnes could!) The dance-pantomime on that tiny stage was picturesquely set. The main character—I recall no others—was a shepherd with a flute.

Perhaps we would have been nearly as enthralled even if he hadn't danced, for this truly beautiful, graceful, and highly gifted shepherd was to achieve a fame not quite the same as Bernhardt's or Duse's, but still very great. He was young, young Ramon Novarro.

Hollywood When Silents Were Golden

Walking home drowsily past fields of nightshade and mustard, and fences strung with passion vine, we looked up at our stars not yet paled by city lights, not yet programmed out of Houston, and it was a luminous outline of the future star Novarro that I saw, not Orion's Belt or the Little Bear.

Just the same, the best of all was set-watching—there you might see a whole galaxy of stars. There was also an advantage we could not ignore. That was *our* spectator sport; outsiders got barred.

Tourists and newcomers often were annoyed. Seeing movies made should be their right, they declared, as with picking an orange from a tree. We explained that if you stopped to pick an orange from a roadside grove out here, you could get shot.

For one orange? they asked.

We begged them to remember what one orange per one thousand visitors would mean. Similarly, if they all got inside studios, casts and crews might be crushed to death. They were not convinced, so we learned to keep still about seeing sets. Year after year, sometimes twice a year, we children went to look at Uncle Cecil's sets.

Almost every Cecil de Mille picture had—as well as a bathtub, for a time his trademark—a resplendent set. Sometimes both. He well knew how much Lizzie and Jakie relished costly trappings of make-believe. He put a moral at the end, but along the way there was idle luxury, preening selfishness, lots of overdress, and some undress.

Mother kept me out of the Aztec palace in *The Woman God Forgot* because she thought the cast was too unclothed, and that nudity was unbecoming to most of the men, but I missed few other of the great de Mille scenes. They were more red-letter on our calendar than the Easter Sunrise Service or the New Year's Day Parade.

There was *We Can't Have Everything*—Moorish, harem, camels; *Adam's Rib*—prehistoric, sylvan, actors wearing animal pelts, and a very young actor in a very small pelt complaining to his mother between takes, "My tail is cold." There

Set-watching

was *Male and Female*, made from James M. Barrie's play *The Admirable Crichton*. Uncle Cecil derived a stunning flashback from poetic lines Barrie had quoted to point up that today's butler might have been yesterday's Darius: "When I was a king in Babylon and you were a Christian slave."

Thomas Meighan, sternly handsome, was the butler and, in the Big Set we attended, the king also. Gloria Swanson was the modern English lady who found herself briefly back in that ancient time (just what time would have combined a king in Babylon with a Christian slave was somewhat vague) and at the mercy—how delightful—of Thomas Meighan. What we enjoyed most, we children anyway, was that tigers prowled the Babylonian palace on chains barely short enough so they couldn't claw the stars.

Later, Thomas Meighan did get clawed. The *Male and Female* company went to the isthmus of Catalina Island, which had a fine curve of tropical, deserted beach, to make sequences in which the butler and the beauty had been castaway. There was a scene in which Thomas Meighan was to work with a leopard he, supposedly, had bagged and slung across his back. The leopard was a real one, drugged. It started to revive during the scene. The actor acted on, just as if paws were not flexing in his back.

Big sets often meant wild animals. In *Fool's Paradise* the grisly menace was afforded by an alligator pit. The villain, a Siamese prince, made a habit of tossing in people he didn't like. From *Fool's Paradise* Mother brought home useful alligator lore. For instance, alligators were lethargic but, their appetites aroused, they could be magically quick at snapping with their jaws or belting with their tails. The idea hypnotized Katie and me, and between shots we sat with our legs hanging in the pit—well above those dreaming snouts, of course, and utterly ignored.

The big set in *Forbidden Fruit* was the ballroom of the castle in the tale of "Cinderella." Agnes Ayres, Cinderella in a huge powdered wig and a mass of glittering and partly see-

through skirt, had to descend a staircase made of glass. Water flowed beneath the stairs which, between the takes, got covered to protect their shine. Walking down them in glass slippers must have needed as much courage as climbing up the walls of Orleans.

At the foot of the stairs Prince Charming waited to kiss Cinderella's hand. Either this Prince Charming didn't have the proper hand or he was somewhere else when time to shoot the insert came, for here Father gave his best performance in a film. It was his small and rather graceful hand that got used, to raise that of Agnes Ayres. He remained her devoted fan and took me to see *her* in *The Sheik*, when everybody else went to see Valentino.

The first *Ten Commandments* had many handsome scenes, but we never saw the shooting of the most astounding one, where the Red Sea parted. This was done by Process, and the Process was a secret. (There were jokes, of course, to the effect that Uncle Cecil tried in vain to get the Red Sea to divide at his command.) New techniques of Process and Effect had to be preserved from poachers, too.

We got our Biblical money's worth when it came to *The King of Kings*, from the span of zebras (striped donkeys?) driven by Judas prior to his stint as an Apostle, to the Crucifixion itself.

A tremendous stage at De Mille Studio was transformed into the Place of the Skull. We who were permitted to look on stood on a catwalk balcony high above but not apart from the tension of the set. This was more than everyday illusion. H. B. Warner, playing Jesus, seemed to step aside and let an idea animate the scene.

For the final moments of the Crucifixion, there could only be one take. This was a breakaway set. When the thunder and lightning rent the sky above Golgotha, rifts were to open in the earth, and stunt men would be swallowed in their depths. Though injuries in stunt work were not common now, there was always risk. Since it would be very hard to put Golgotha

Set-watching

back together again after the breakaway, and no one wanted to take extra chances with the stunt men, the action would get shot just once.

We gripped the railing edge as the signal came, the sky (a cyclorama under lights) turned dark, the earth heaved, and the actors fell to their knees, cried to heaven, or were catapulted into clefts. There was such a whirl of turbulence, cloud, and terror that, though old enough to know better, I would not have been surprised if the catwalk and the stage, and in fact the world, had gone tumbling down.

Lo, I am with you always (Matt. 28:20), were the comforting Bible words across a city skyline at the end of the picture when it was released. But they were not there at the shooting of the breakaway and it seemed to us that we were staring into endless chaos.

The last big de Mille sets I visited were during what we thought of as Uncle Cecil's Babylonian exile, after De Mille Studio closed, at Metro-Goldwyn-Mayer. He went there to spend two years in a charming office-bungalow but an atmosphere of Show Us! At least that's what Mother thought; she did not find MGM a friendly lot. She sprained an ankle, asked permission (seldom granted to those lower than producer rank) to be driven through the studio gates—her office was two blocks away, inside—and received it after she was well and her contract had run out.

Nonetheless, I wriggled in to set-watch once on *Madame Satan*, where a dirigible (memory of Mercury Aviation?) was supposed to catch on fire and the guests at Madame Satan's masquerade to jump into a net. Then I stood by at the mine disaster scene in *Dynamite*.

In *Dynamite*, Kay Johnson, a coolly pleasant star with a little of the manner of Aunt Constance, was a spoiled heiress who married Charles Bickford, on Death Row, to fulfill the conditions of a will. Then Bickford, who of course turned out to be as innocent of crime as Katie's dog, got set free, and insisted the heiress live with him as a simple miner's wife.

This was something less than convincing as a plot, and the theme song, "How Am I To Know?" had a more lasting impact than the picture. The plaintive lyric by Dorothy Parker, poet and wit, was actually *sung* in the picture. *Dynamite* was on the cusp of the change from silents to talkies and was made in both a silent and a sound version. Some theatres were prepared with sound-reproducing equipment; some as yet were not. Russ Columbo, who seemed destined to become a singing Valentino, but died in an accident with a gun, did the singing. Twenty years later, in another film, Ava Gardner furnished a reprise.

The finale of *Dynamite* showed the principals trapped by a cave-in of a mine. Safely out of camera range, I was waiting for the action to begin when I decided it was time to throw away my gum. I seldom chewed gum, partly because my parents thought the habit odious, partly because chewing got so dull and called for so much jawbone energy. I chucked my wad into a brazier which was being used to warm the set. To my dismay, it seemed at once that smoke began to rise.

Action!

Charles Bickford and Kay Johnson, blocked by tons of rock, listened for a sound of rescue, and then studied the canary in its cage to see whether they were running out of air. I studied the brazier. Was "my" smoke going to drift into the scene, adding an unscheduled menace? Had I spoiled the take?

Happily, when rescuers burst through the rock, light flooded in undimmed by smoke and I was not disgraced on that last Big Set.

I saw a lot more movies shot, but no more de Mille spectacles. After MGM there were none for a year or so, till Uncle Cecil went back to Paramount—to *The Sign of the Cross*, the second *Ten Commandments*, and *The Greatest Show on Earth*.

This time Mother didn't go with him. She went to Fox, to continue a long, happy partnership with Bertram Millhauser.

XXVI
Dress and Undress

Other movies besides Uncle Cecil's had spectacle—*Hell's Angels* for one. It had its dash of the risqué, too. There was a scene where Jean Harlow brought her escort home after a gala evening, and excused herself to change into "something more comfortable." She had on an evening dress which pretty well confirmed the rumor about no brassiere. She changed into a bathrobe which covered up much more of her. Wasn't that ridiculous? I thought. Surely the less covered the more comfortable.

While my reaction wasn't very relevant to the basic meaning of the scene, it did reflect a growing tendency towards undress both in me and the times. Mother, in her jousting with the censors, was far less concerned with their desire to paste fig leaves over nudity than their plastering of cabbage leaves on facts. But for some time a quiet underground, not of nudists in a current sense, had been waging war to wear and enjoy plain skin. Parents of one of my friends even roamed their home without clothes "so the children wouldn't grow up self-conscious about the human form."

I quailed at this (what would you be except self-conscious over your parents' form?) but delighted in a story Bertram Millhauser told about his introduction to the movies. Mill—he preferred even his wife to call him Mill—was brilliant, sensitive, warm-hearted, and had permanently startled eyes. We

wondered if they got that way the day he met Pearl White.

He had grown up on the New York East Side and married his delightful Olga there. (She came to the United States with her family, from Minsk. It was suggested to her that she should Americanize her name. She did—to Olga Alice.) His first job was dock work. *Catch hold.* Underage and underweight, he caught hold of several tons of cargo before he got his chance to write. He was hired to work on *The Perils of Pauline*, the most famous of all serials, with the most famous of all serial stars.

When Mill checked in at the Long Island studio from which Pauline sallied out to hang from trestles or be trussed in front of buzz saws, he was ordered to report to Miss White's bungalow. He hurried there with beating heart, knocked, and was invited in. His heart almost stopped. Pearl White lay on a couch with nothing on. She wasn't being a temptress, she was just relaxing. And this wasn't even Hollywood!

Out in the West, relaxing without clothes—or with few— had the advantage of the sun, which some people had begun to think was therapeutic. As early as 1909, a father took his ailing son to the Palm Springs desert. Somewhat later my friend Isabelle's aunt, Cornelia, struggling with muscle aches and pains, moved to the same spot. She made herself a sun-bathing machine of canvas and poles where she spent a part of every day.

Palm Springs was a quail-crossing then, with far fewer humans than quail. Louella Parsons, the rising gossip columnist, went there for a rest. It proved restful, indeed; the chief daily stimulation was some poetry reading after dinner in the one hotel. Even the local lady wrangler attended this, though she usually fell asleep with her boots on a chair. Learning there was a neighbor also from the city, Louella Parsons paid Cornelia a call.

Like Mill, she knocked, as well as one can on canvas. Cornelia shouted that she wasn't dressed. The visitor must have

Dress and Undress

assumed this was a phrase like "I haven't got a thing to wear." She walked inside the sunbathing machine. Cornelia not only wasn't dressed, she had by then been tanned into mahogany. Louella Parsons wasn't shocked as Mill had been shocked, but so much of such a color did appear bizarre!

To the hotel, though, Louella was bizarre. She had brought along a secretary, male. Things "like that" weren't being done in Palm Springs. It took all Cornelia's tact, as go-between, to prevent Louella's eviction, through convincing the hotel that newspaper business associations were not things "like that."

Didn't so much sun take something out of you? people asked from under scarves and broad-brimmed hats.

Apparently not. Thirty years later, finished with her work as wife and mother, Cornelia Runyon began sculpturing in rock. No one but the Maya ever shaped a coiled granite serpent as well or made a more soaring bird of quartz.

But the first time we went to Palm Springs, we were *overdressed*.

In an early letter East, Mother remarked that people actually did sometimes travel to the desert out of choice. It wasn't just a barren expanse with bleaching bones. Still, it took a new arrival from the East to get us there. She was just getting accustomed to her desk in Culver City under that pickle sign, when Mrs. Joseph Grismer moved into a house two hills away from Argyle Avenue, on Whitley Heights. Whitley Heights was a breakneck, atmospheric, elegant hump of villas opposite the Hollywood Bowl.

The late Joseph Grismer had been writer-producer of the play *Way Down East*, which wrung cataracts of tears from theatre audiences long before it was an equally affecting Griffith movie. Mrs. Grismer had been the actress Olive Thorne. We never saw her on the stage, but in a drawing room she could charm, amuse, or insult with the merest look or phrase, and sometimes all at the same time.

She brought West with her "little" Olive, her daughter,

who was slightly younger than I, and her son by an earlier marriage, Joe Harper, who was slightly older. Not too much, I kept saying to myself. Most of the time from then on some of our group of girls, all of our group of girls, or at least one of us, was to be in love with Joe.

We were ringed round with what Lizzie (if not Jakie) thought of as the world's most personable men. Not enough of them, of course—even in Hollywood there were fewer men than girls. Still, we knew a good many, and we certainly had more acquaintance with sleek Latin types or blond gods than they did in Boise, Idaho. After all, the Latin types and blond gods rushed from Boise to Hollywood. Some of these young men were fun. Some of them were bright. We were not immune to their looks and their behavior, enriched by the parts they played or hoped to play.

That was the trouble—parts were always foremost in the actor's mind, or we thought they were, which was as bad. Your rival was Corinne Griffith, Barbara LaMarr, Marie Prevost— or tomorrow's interview. The young men you began to know who didn't act, but photographed, or cut, or wanted to direct, still belonged more to the set or the cutting room than to you.

This was not true of Joe. He didn't want to act, direct, or get into the movies at all. Nor did he belong to any of us for a good long while, but the rivalry made quite a change—what he wanted was a ranch. By the same token he was not the kind of Easterner who came to be amused by our crudity, tossing off our landscape with a shrug and our culture with a laugh. Joe gave us a broad smile, showing dimples; with his Eastern manners he had Western legs (six feet long in Levis) and perhaps a fortune, too. All this when most of us were in our teens!

Mrs. Grismer, too, occasionally shrugged about the West and about us girls. The lipstick we put on—the high heels! What for? Joe had been engaged in New York (both families had said "too young"), and the girl he left behind wasn't

Dress and Undress

merely pretty, but sweet, affectationless—although the child of a really eminent man, Hamlin Garland. To many eyes Hamlin Garland was the dean of American letters since publishing his *Son of the Middle Border*, which abruptly put the Middle West on the literary map. Just then his daughter Constance, pretty and sweet without lipstick or high heels, was illustrating his next book. What made us be ornate?

There was no quick answer.

Fortunately Mrs. Grismer switched to something else. Ornateness could be tolerated in a landscape—or perhaps she wanted to get broken in for Joe's ranch: she suggested New Year's in Palm Springs. We all thought it a first-rate idea. She and Father hit it off much as he and Bibi had. He and Joe got on famously. Any age difference between "little" Olive and myself wouldn't show on horseback. Mother was to find she liked the desert under Mt. San Jacinto just as much as she had liked looking at it from above. Cecilia went with us, too.

Palm Springs in 1925 had one sandy main street looped with palms and *two* main hotels. We stayed in the newer one; Mrs. Grismer wasn't really roughing it. She and Mother put on hats with brims and sat beneath a smoke tree while we rode. Riding at Palm Springs in those days was like loping through the finest desert painting you had ever seen. A half mile from the town, you were aware of nothing but hills, towering nearby, floating, farther off, ringing the plain of sand and brush with sunset colors as unbelievable as those in the tails of Siamese fighting fish. Perhaps there was a link, in the latent menace of the lovely desert and the lovely fish.

I was growing up to be a victim of all horses—an animal aged thirty-two would slowly bolt with me—but you couldn't mind even being bolted with, out there. We jogged home, a little dazed, as it grew dark.

"Aunt" Helen Belknap had been found by Mrs. Grismer and Mother, staying at the other hotel with her daughter Isabelle, and Virginia, the veteran of the Universal–Indian

rides. Mrs. Grismer and Mother had invited Aunt Helen for cocktails. Aunt Helen invited all of us to go out with her hand-in-hand into the brush to welcome the New Year. It was gracious on her part, for she didn't think Palm Springs at all the place for cocktails and had been upset because we dressed for dinner. It could ruin the desert which, like Constance Garland, so far was affectationless, if not actually sweet.

We walked into the plain of sand and brush, by moonlight now, and Aunt Helen seemed a trifle upset, too, that Joe and Cecilia really did hold hands. However, as midnight came, we were properly hushed—not a noisemaker for miles—and we gave our silent wishes to the stars. Then Cecilia and I talked in our room till three. I think I told her all my secrets, and she told me some of hers, though not what she had wished.

We went back to Hollywood with a swish of Mother's evening cape of black crepe de Chine and monkey fur. Since then, no doubt, enough mink has been worn at the spa to wrap three times round the world. Did Our Overdressing Spoil Palm Springs?

On an afternoon at Catalina Island, Joe and I were perilously overdressed. We had gone riding on the hot, sagey, almost savage, inland trails. After we returned our horses to the stable, we decided to canoe to our hotel, around the point. We were well out into choppy water, leaving Avalon Bay where the bells pealed "Avalon" for every ferry that arrived or left, when we realized we could easily capsize. We both had on the junior lead weights of our Western boots.

We rounded the point with a certain extra zest, whisking by the bobbing yachts in the St. Catherine cove. Even I, who treasured every moment with Joe, was happy when we hit the beach. In the movies such peril would have propelled us right into each other's arms. Joe pulled off my boots and hurried to change clothes. His girl was due to join him, from a bobbing yacht.

An hour later, up in Mother's room, I looked out on what

Dress and Undress

would have made a charming sequence for a musical. A launch swept to the hotel dock. A ravishingly handsome, dark young man leaped out and gave his hand to a beautiful blonde girl, Joe's girl. This was another Constance, Constance Howard, not much older than I, playing the lead in that yachtsman's film.

"See—there's Richard Barthelmess," I called to Mother, as the dark young man embraced the whole hotel—the whole island!—with his smile. *Something* could be salvaged out of bystandings.

"I've seen," said Mother, who was playing solitaire, interested not in the star of *Way Down East* and *Broken Blossoms*, but in a trapped ace. "He was pretty wishy-washy in *The Fighting Blade*."

XXVII
Blue Is the Night

1925—We all went constantly to *No, No, Nanette,* the musical comedy with such cheerful songs, "Tea for Two" and "I Want to Be Happy." Not that we hadn't learned the words the first time round, but that Billy Buckland fell in love with the ingenue. She had to be substantially older than he; he was fourteen. He was also still angel eyed, and she (and her husband) graciously joined us all so he could gaze at her more closely, at the beach.

1925—I passed my driver's examination with a flair. During the test, a streetcar ran into me. The streetcar was severely blamed. Streetcars seemed in training to be juggernauts, just then. The year before, Gene Stratton Porter, author of the immensely popular *Girl of the Limberlost,* had moved to California to produce her own films, and been killed when a streetcar struck her limousine.

1925 was the year Cecilia and Margaret got through with H.S.G. The school had a senior class play every year. That year there were two. The double helping came from the fact that now we had a real theatre for our use, a movie theatre managed by a classmate's father, which he kindly made available for matinees. Margaret was going to do more acting later. As far as I was concerned, 1925 was Cecilia's acting year.

First she was in *Twelfth Night,* as Malvolio. There was a scene which called for her to wear a nightshirt. Uncle Cecil lent her one. Nightshirts were far out of fashion then. What

a mark of fatherly esteem for this famous man, wrongly or rightly linked in the public mind with alluring women, to let his daughter spell out his sleepwear habit there in cambric, with his monogram!

The second play was *David Garrick*, and Cecilia was Garrick. There was a tipsy scene in which she had to waver round the stage flourishing a lighted candle. Cecilia had rehearsed it all in middy and skirt. When she got to the scene at the matinee, the candle set fire to her eighteenth-century lace cuff. From my seat in the back row I could see Uncle Cecil, down in front, start to climb over the footlights. Cecilia blew the fire out. We went backstage to compliment her coolness. She explained that she had known the cuff was bound to ignite, but had had no doubt that she could cope.

No wonder Father wished I could be more like Cecilia! The most striking thing I did was carry one end of a flower arch when she graduated. Again we tramped from the barn to the lawn chanting "Ancient of Days" and tramped back with Kipling's "Recessional" and its somewhat forbidding words about progress "through seas dryshod and weary wastes bewildering." Margaret won the tennis trophy and the French medal and shared the scholarship award. Cecilia won the citizenship prize, which covered everything else. Everything else in school, that is. Next day she got three Firsts and a Grand Championship in a Pasadena horse show.

Two years later there were frightful winter floods; *The King of Kings* opened at Grauman's Chinese—I cried my own flood ("It was so b-beautiful") and looked so soggy Up At The House afterwards that Uncle Cecil wondered if he had left out the Resurrection; and *I* graduated. I won six of seven possible prizes, but my parents helped me not to lose my head. Mother shrugged and said it really was a small school. Father didn't say a word. Much later Joe Harper remarked that Father really almost burst with pride, out of my sight, and I challenged Father: I had thought he wasn't even pleased!

"That's the way it ought to be," he said.

What really touched Mother, during the graduation ceremony, was that we sang—how much we did sing!—an air from *Martha* with words she claimed had been written for her own Chelsea High Commencement. "In the harbor we've been sheltered/Gathering strength to glide away...." There were tears in her eyes. How odd, to care about what happened forty years ago!

Things got odder. This was the season when I learned about the William de Mille divorce.

In spite of all the outside talk about blasé, if not downright rakehell, Hollywood, our Hollywood was shocked. Good, intelligent, piquant Aunt Anna—good, intelligent, astringent Uncle William! Divorce in itself was still considered bad; how much worse with friends; how much worse when there was family! The idea that an unhappy home might injure children as much as a broken one was as yet hardly known. Two sets of parents would confuse, neglect or possibly spoil children.

At my age level, the divorce not only seemed sad, it seemed absurd. Couldn't people with almost grown-up children make the best of things, for their few remaining years?

The William de Milles plainly thought they couldn't. The divorce proceedings began, and our Hollywood took sides. It was the old "London Bridge Is Falling Down," with harsh words between the teams. Veda Buckland and "Aunt" Mildred Smith, mother of my Japanese tutors Mary and Caroline, quite fiercely chose Aunt Anna. A few studio people just as strongly held to Uncle William, who was known to be intending to remarry.

Mother surprised me. I would have expected her to say that divorce broke at least two family commandments (not to hurt a child, never to betray a friend) but, along with Uncle Cecil's household, ours remained impartial. Mother knew the future Mrs. William de Mille, writer Clara Beranger, who had worked on scripts for Uncle William since 1921. Mother

Blue Is the Night

liked Aunt Anna, but she liked Clara, too. From those early days when she had found out so much about the craft of motion pictures, thanks to Uncle William, she thought she understood what the comradeship of someone sharing his film interest would mean. Aunt Anna's mind was still a great deal on her father, Henry George. Mother saw no one to blame.

But that didn't help with social life. You had to be careful about what you said, about whom you gathered as your guests; and then, just after my graduation, Clara Beranger's daughter Frances, who had lived in the East, came to visit her. Frances was a tall, lovely, fair-skinned brunette with blue eyes. Was she also thin-skinned? Mother thought it probable. Why didn't I find this a chance to make a friend and show Frances around, with an eye to doors that might slam and gates that could be closed?

This was also the time that Margaret de Mille and I had chosen to be friends. She was staying with some cousins of her mother and rehearsing in light summer fare at the respected Pasadena Playhouse.

Nearly every day I went to Pasadena with Margaret. Nearly every day I swam with Frances. For a span of weeks I engaged in a form of double life and was far from proud of it. Thanks to Mother, I could see that they were not easy weeks for Frances; I already gathered they were hard for Margaret; they were often fun but always hazardous for me. Perhaps it would have been pleasing to deceive the German High Command or the Russian Secret Police. It was something else to tell half-truths to friends. If either one found out I had just finished shopping with the other, no lives would get lost, but someone I cared for might be hurt.

I kept my mouth shut and felt like a sneak.

I also kept up my jaunts from girl to girl. Frances and her mother had a bungalow at the Garden of Alla, the bewitching hotel made from the estate of Alla Nazimova. I would leave Frances in the pool—sunlight drifting like gold dust through

the clear water (you could definitely see the bottom here)—and meet Margaret for early dinner before her play. Sometimes we made the still partly rural drive to Pasadena alone, sometimes with two of her most fascinating friends, Claude Fielding, who told tales of mystery and imagination about growing up in India (it really made no difference whether they were true), and stalwart, amiable Jimmy Beard who told quieter but funny stories, too. Had he only told me about food! I grew up to be a culinary moron. He went on to be the gastronomic genius James Beard, maestro of hors d'oeuvres and picnic barbecue.

At the Pasadena Playhouse, I watched Margaret make up. She heated mascara till it looked like tar, an alchemy I wished that I had known before, and built double coronets around her eyes. Then I watched the play—*The Devil's Den*—probably a dozen times. Lloyd Nolan, not yet touched by the movies in which he would have a long, substantial career, was the star. My leanings were towards the villain, though, who was looked upon backstage as "difficult." Like difficult, though spellbinding, Jetta Goudal, he experienced an awkward moment. He had to be discovered hanging in one scene. The curtain then was quickly closed and he got hauled down—the position, though not strangling, was troublesome. On the last night of the play, there was some delay in hauling him down.

Margaret's part made few dramatic demands, but she did have a chance to wear fancy dress (there was a masked ball in *The Devil's Den*) in joyful reprise of our childhood gatherings. Then she left for New York, where she played a lead in *Green Grow the Lilacs* (the future *Oklahoma!*) opposite a future great charmer of the screen, Franchot Tone.

Somewhat later, during evenings after work, Mother wrote another book.

Since *The Turned About Girls*, she had had published—in 1927—a collection of her rhymed children's plays. But her book in 1929 was no juvenile. It was about a writer who required a divorce from his good and loyal wife so that he could

Blue Is the Night

marry someone else. The writer was *not* also a director of motion pictures. The wife was *not* an intellectual nor yet the daughter of a famous man. The Other Woman in the book was not the writer's business colleague but a pampered middle-aged coquette, so the plot was not as much related to the growing apart of mature people as to the misfortune of a middle-aged aberration.

Just the same, Mother worried. She never did believe in copying verbatim out of life; still, life was bound to find its way through even her imagination. Like me and my half-truths with Margaret and Frances, she chose a subterfuge. A pseudonym was tacked on the book. She said it was because the Eastern critics were unmerciful to Hollywood writers. (So now she was from Hollywood! Not to hear her long New England a's. Not to read her Radcliffe-structured prose.) The jacket of the book *Their Own Desire* gave Sarita Fuller as the author's name.

It was a combination of the atmosphere of the Southwest with a family surname; it was also a mistake, from the point of view of anonymity, if not the point of view of sales. At the Hollywood Bookstore, where "all Hollywood" browsed, the friendly owners quickly pointed to "Mrs. Flebbe's new book." Surely only Mother could have been so innocent as to suppose that her secret would be kept, and not to realize that a bogus name merely "confirmed" the guess that *Their Own Desire* was an exposé.

Two of the biggest stars competed for the movie rights. On a Warner Brothers set, Joan Crawford was overheard telling her bridegroom, Douglas Fairbanks, Jr., how much she wanted to be the beleaguered heroine, the writer's daughter tortured with love for the Other Woman's son. Norma Shearer got the part—she had an advantage about parts; she was married to her studio's head. *Their Own Desire* had a lovely theme song ("Blue Is the Night") which, like "How Am I to Know" in *Dynamite*, survived the film.

XXVIII

Up at the House

The drizzly morning when I graduated out of H.S.G.—graduation was the only June day in Southern California when it rained—Mrs. Grismer, little Olive, and Joe had been absent, in New York. Soon from New York came a wedding invitation. Joe had seen the girl he left behind four years ago, and this time he had conquered.

I stared at the invitation, then out at the flower fields, rising in pastel steps towards Mt. Hollywood as if the world would walk right on. It did. Our new automatic record player finished "Two Black Crows" and dropped "Sundown" on the table. I hadn't liked "Sundown" much before. I hated it now.

But I didn't cry. There turned out to be no tears. Being in love with Joe had belonged with being fourteen. Now I was sixteen.

So what else did you feel, as you "Gather[ed] strength to glide away" from H. S. G.?

Relief, of course. Not that being in school had been bad—it had been long; ten years! If you hadn't straggled in, at midyear, and been accelerated through the Montessori class (or through its backwash—there were two opinions as to this), you would have sat through twelve. Ten years of nine months, mostly nine o'clock to three o'clock, though basketball or batiks could make it eight to four. Eighteen hundred days of changing classes by the bell, always the same bell. Mother hadn't, at

Up At The House

least, worked for just one studio! (She had, in fact, planned carefully so I would be spared the waste in time and energy of changing schools; she couldn't do that well about the studios.) I had a touch of claustrophobia. Everyone agreed I should relax and take deep breaths. The air I deeply breathed was that of Laughlin Park.

My last spring at H. S. G. was our last spring at Argyle Avenue. We moved, just down the hill from Up At The House. By that time the Cecil de Milles had lived in Laughlin Park almost ten years, but the day they went there still loomed clear to me.

Knowing they had bought a big white house on a hill, with a view, Bibi drove us for a look. We found such a house, its doors open, nobody at home. We were half way through the rooms, talking about how different, in their new surroundings, well-known chairs and tables looked, when it began to dawn on us that we had entered the wrong house.

Let's not panic, Bibi indicated. In my heart I believed she longed to run just as much as I. But we made an exit of great dignity, so that watching neighbors wouldn't take us for thieves, piled into the Scripps-Booth—Bibi's car then—and, at a punishing speed of thirty m.p.h., raced for home.

On the second try we did find the right house, in such a maze of greenery we always believed Laughlin Park had been a nursery. Certainly the winding drives looked as though laid out with wheelbarrows. There was a hairpin curve where the uninitiated driver had to back up; the In thing, in visiting the House, was *not* to have to back up.

The big sweep of grounds—wilderness at first—was to the rear. We played on the front lawn when we were small. Mother was impressed with our impromptu dancing there. She wrote East, *Cecilia dances with the grace of a wooden doll, but much dramatic fervor. She likes to do things like the death of Carmen, in which she stabs herself with a table knife. Nancy Adams dances conscientiously. The two little Wm. de Milles, Agnes*

and Margaret, are very clever, graceful, and full of imagination. Agnes, aged ten, is really wonderful.

Mother attended the ballet only for my sake. I was once appalled to find her asleep (after a hard day's work) during *The Dying Swan*. But concerning Agnes she had dance judgment.

When I went to play alone with Cecilia, we didn't dance, but the dramatic fervor remained. Mother believed we acted out only Cecil de Mille movie plots, usually *Joan the Woman*, with Cecilia as Joan and me in the other parts. Perhaps we hadn't the heart to tell her that we mostly made up Westerns. The de Milles kept a stable at the bottom of the hill, a perfect spot for Noble Cowboy roles. We escaped Indians and captured horse thieves through the stalls, into the loft, out the windows, and across the horses' backs. Sometimes we even rode.

There was no trace of the stable by 1927. Just about on its site, Father built our house. He was selling residential lots in Laughlin Park, so the house was a demonstrator. Mother probably would have preferred a Tudor cottage, but she got a Spanish villa. It was quite a handsome pile, with a fat tower and a winding stair, created by a former German court architect. From the entrance hall—a wild extravagance in space except that it set off an antique bench Father bought from Valentino's estate—you looked in four directions at a pretty view.

To the west, beyond some trees, was Jack Dempsey's house, same architect. Father sold the property to the famous boxer and his wife, Estelle Taylor, who had been the headstrong Miriam, sister of Moses, in the first *Ten Commandments*. To the north, we had the Japanese flower fields. South, beyond our back patio, Mrs. Grismer built another California Spanish house; then so did Joe and Connie Harper; then so did Connie's family, the Hamlin Garlands. East was all de Mille land, gardens, garages, tennis court, and pool. We could walk Up To The House in five minutes, and almost daily did.

It had lost none of its magic with familiarity—not even any

Up At The House

of its size, as the front door swung wide and Frederick, the butler, let us in. He never frowned and hardly smiled. The foyer gleamed, dustless. On the left were stairs which Katie never climbed without an arm behind her back. She said this was to make sure of not getting stabbed, a childhood quirk or perhaps a joke—with Katie, who looked like an exquisite small Richard Barthelmess and had an epidemic laugh, how could you tell?

There was one stair on the right, down into the living room. A dog still spraddled on the hearth, not Sloppy now, but Angie, who was pure white, with a touch of blackness in his heart. Angie snored horribly and Uncle Cecil sometimes banished him from runnings, which were in the Other House. Angie would then trot upstairs, select a spot in the bedroom right above Uncle Cecil's chair, and snore through the floor.

Next to Angie, the most decorative object in the living room was an Indian box on the piano, crusted over with semiprecious stones. It was a gift from some Eastern potenate, a glorious prop, or both, and it flashed against the sober blackness of the piano rather like the one brilliant ring Uncle Cecil wore with his sober clothes. Uncle Cecil once had lost the ring, from a dock at Catalina, while shooting *Feet of Clay*. A diver found it on the ocean floor when the tide was low. Perhaps Uncle Cecil *could* have parted the Red Sea?

Anyway, his style awed fellow tycoons. The men who, with him, had all but invented movies were not quite, as alleged, peddlers who could neither read nor write, but they hadn't had his cultivated father nor his polished mother. After a party with them on the de Mille yacht, Father said, "Cecil is the great gentleman Louis B. Mayer wishes he could be."

Up At The House, I had one experience with Uncle Cecil's gentlemanly sarcasm. It was before we moved to the Park; I was naive and young and pleased to sit beside him at the dinner table. On my other side was Katie. She had just come home from boarding school, and my joy at our reunion even overcame my interest in the new treat at our plates, macadamia

nuts. During the first course, I hardly ate at all as I attempted to catch Katie up on all the news. I didn't think I was being rude; I supposed everyone was chattering in pairs.

But they had stopped. Suddenly I felt the silence. Uncle Cecil, it appeared, was in a mood for table-wide discussion. Bending towards me, he said, "If it's so interesting, Evelyn, perhaps you'll let us all in on it."

I did not then know he was celebrated for his sarcasm, which had reduced phalanxes of underlings to tears. I thought he was sincere, so I let him in. If he wanted to hear how brunette Mary Anita Loos (whose aunt Anita Loos made famous certain blondes) claimed to be of Egyptian blood, or how Patty Lighton (whose mother wrote and whose father produced) managed, with her melting eyes, to collect a bangle bracelet from every youth who took her out, that was certainly all right with me.

Uncle Cecil paid me back—not that he intended to—a few years further on. It was a Sunday running with the usual guests—Nancy Adams and her mother, Julia Faye, Jeanie Macpherson, Uncle Cecil's secretary, and ourselves. We had all grown up enough to have wine at dinner, if we wished, and Nancy and Cecilia, at least, would be joined at running time by various young men.

I have no recollection of what the picture was that night, for though I grimly kept my eyes on it, I was aware only of a young man seated just across the homemade aisle. He was near the top of my quite extensive list of captivating males. He was, otherwise, an almost unknown actor by the name of Larry Kent. He lived at the Hollywood Athletic Club, where I had sometimes glimpsed him, now that, post H.S.G., I spent so many hours there. He had been in one picture, *Hangman's House*, which I had seen. He was *wonderful* in it, I thought—though not very good, which was different. One of Cecilia's beaux was his closest friend, so I had learned he was a loner who liked boats. Though I hated boats, I was a loner, which seemed the basis for a fine relationship.

Up At The House

However, when he arrived at the House, unexpectedly (at least to me), I was ill-prepared. Our entire conversation so far had been "How Do You Do?"

Then the picture ended. He leaned across the aisle and asked me something. How I liked it, I suppose.

I was burning to reply, really to engage in talk with this fascinating being who appeared to me so perfect, from his plain brown hair to his costly buckskin shoes. But after a running, only Uncle Cecil spoke. He didn't look at pictures every Sunday just to be amused, but to keep abreast of movies as a whole. We saw his films, his friends' films, rival films, and even foreign films. We also were there primarily for business, to give him our reactions if he asked for them.

First he might turn to Aunt Constance, Mother, or Jeanie, then to the others, one by one. Every opinion had its worth for him. But we never opened our mouths out of turn. I could not break the rule, risk the sarcasm—it had been explained to me now—or, above all, let Larry Kent impair his chances with director de Mille.

So I never answered him. Uncle Cecil's questions parted us for good.

Cecilia did invite me to stay on for cocoa with Larry and his friend. The omens seemed wrong. I walked home down the hill with my parents. It really didn't matter where we moved or whom we had as friends, I was still afflicted with the state of being seventeen. Unlucky at love, lucky at cards? Next time I played poker Up At The House, I was dealt a royal flush.

XXIX
Shoulder-rubbing, and Other Tales

On the other hand, I at least *met* Larry Kent. There was a surprising number of people in Hollywood that I didn't meet.

I couldn't help seeing most of them. We went to the same places. We had lunch at Henry's, the Victor Hugo, Musso's, the Derby, the Ancient Mariner, and the Gotham. The Ancient Mariner was done up with fish net, harpoons, and painted quotations from the Coleridge poem of that name. I liked the poem (loved the restaurant) but felt somewhat wrongly placed under the lines "Water, water everywhere, nor any drop to drink" in a cozy booth supplied with iced tea and a sparkling water pitcher. I switched my affections to the Gotham when I found that Joe Harper, having given up his ranch, ate his lunch there every day—a turkey sandwich and a champagne split.

We went to the Cotton Club, the Montmartre, the Biltmore, the Cocoanut Grove, and Agua Caliente for the horse races.

I was at the Montmartre when Alice White, the perfect flapper image starring with Arthur Lake (whom I did know, a little bit) in *Harold Teen*, missed her chair and sat down on the floor. "Imagine my embarrassment," said Alice White. Real live *Harold Teen*.

I was at the Grove, among the artificial palms and artificial monkeys with their electric eyes, when Gretchen Young—as my friends called her—won the dance contest. This made it seem so apt, not much later, when her first starring movie (not

as Gretchen Young but as Loretta Young) was titled *The Kiss Waltz.*

I was having creme de menthe, my compromise between "I drink" and "I don't drink," at Caliente when Drew Percy, whose sister Eileen had been an early star, sat down at a nearby table. He was attractive, too; his sister had married one of Mill's best friends. But I never did meet Drew.

I was at the races closer to Los Angeles when Lupe Velez strolled by, arm in arm with Gary Cooper, no small feat since he was a yard or so taller than she. I got covered with sand at the beach when a couple of boys threw Betty Bronson ("Peter Pan") into the surf.

This didn't add up to all-my-best-friends-are-celebrities any more than if I had lived in Whitefish. In fact, I was less able than if I had been a rank outsider to walk over and join in. How ridiculous could you be, after growing up in Hollywood, to behave like a fan? Yes, but wasn't walking over simply neighborly?

By the time I thought that out, whoever I would have liked to join—and let's face it, it was not really Betty Bronson and Lupe Velez, but Gary Cooper and those boys—would have walked away.

I had some near misses.

Probably the star we liked the longest was Ronald Colman. That tenderness, that irony, that understated gallantry enthralled us from *The White Sister* right through *Bulldog Drummond.* The day I discovered Father planned an overnight trip with Ronald Colman to look over real estate, I thought light might break at last in my Enchanted Wood.

I began to work on Father carefully. I knew neither pouting nor pleading would get me asked along. Perhaps if I touched the subject lightly—if I said it was absurd to live in Hollywood and not know Ronald Colman, like being in Paris and not seeing the art treasures of the Louvre—wouldn't that succeed?

No.

Father didn't let the subject of the trip come up again. He may have canceled it, or compressed it to a day. Ronald Colman stayed tantalizingly near. He bought a house Mrs. Grismer had owned, hallowed for me by some hours I had spent reading to Joe when he had a cold. It was never re-hallowed by a call on Colman. We still lived on Argyle Avenue then. I could see the Colman roof. I never saw him closer than a movie screen. He was the big one that got away.

John Barrymore, so thrilling, one leg and all, in *The Sea Beast*, was an old friend of Mrs. Grismer. He had married Dolores Costello, who was gorgeous. Why would I hope to meet him? Why not? But though he used to drop in at the Grismer house in Laughlin Park, it was not in search of youthful adulation. I was never hailed across the patio for a bracing chat about whales, or the New York stage.

Tullio Carminati was a guest at one of Mrs. Grismer's teas. I did meet him, but he looked exactly like a mature Italian count (which he was), and I didn't know till afterwards that he had been the star of the racy play *Strictly Dishonorable*, and it was still later that he played opposite Grace Moore in one of the first successful singing films, *One Night of Love*. Anyway, even I did not suppose I would have had much in common with an "old" Italian count.

Would I have a lot in common with a movie star?

My parents certainly hoped not. Also, for the good of my soul, they (particularly Father) emphasized why should a movie star be interested in meeting me? Father was neither a producer nor a director. He was not a millionaire, though he still hoped to be. Mother had no casting influence, or not very much. This approach was not a cheering one. Actors aren't good enough for you—but you aren't good enough for them.

It could hardly be bad for me to meet Mary Pickford, though, and think how that would perk the conversation up, next time I visited my real, New England aunt! Mary Pickford was one of the closest friends of Winifred and Dustin Farnum.

Shoulder-rubbing, and Other Tales

We had dinner at their house. I wore evening shoes dyed to match my dress; they had shrunk, and I was in the vulgar plight Mother deplored in comedies. I hobbled round the house admiring the new burglar alarms and a splendid photo of Our Mary propped in bed among embroidered cushions—tenderly inscribed. That's as close to her as I got.

I would have liked to look like Norma Shearer. (*Then* who wouldn't want to meet me!) Her sister looked like her, and came to dinner at our house with her husband Howard Hawks, the director on Mother's current script. But Norma didn't come.

One of the aviators we had known at Mercury Aviation was Marcel de Sano, a Rumanian ace who flew for France in World War I. He was slender, with wavy black hair (almost a marcel) and in his Latin way—if you were dark haired then, you got labeled Latin—very good looking. *Only he was married*, a key phrase to us all. We were not a generation of born home wreckers. His very pretty wife Peggy seemed shy, though she had had the courage to be a news photographer in New York. She also had the courage presently to divorce Marcel, who was later to be referred to as a "bastard" by F. Scott Fitzgerald, who had to write with him on a film called *Redhead*.

Peggy stayed a good friend, and when she married again—the editor of *The New York Daily Mirror*—she brought us details of week ends spent at San Simeon, William Randolph Hearst's great castle and, in those days, the most fabulous place anyone could go. She also talked about her brother, George Nolan, who had toured in *Abie's Irish Rose*. I knew that he fell from the stage once and broke an arm and went on with the show. I knew that when he reached the bottom of his luck, he bought a bunch of flowers and just looked at them. I knew he was the best of brothers. But I never knew *him*, either then or when his luck improved and he became movie star George Brent.

Finally, perhaps, there was Lew Ayres.

After we had all seen *All Quiet on the Western Front*, it wasn't the heartbreaking performance of schoolmate Ben

Alexander that brought us back for a second and third time (Ben was still too *young*), but that of newcomer Lew Ayres. Almost everyone I knew, knew him. I went dozens of places where he was expected or had just that minute left. I heard long descriptions of his personality. My acquaintance stayed at secondhand.

What a lot we heard!

Some stories came right off the set. In the days when a child's earnings were paid to his parents, and no law decreed that so much as a nickel must go to the child himself, a director we knew took the father of a boy star to one side and promised to beat him down to boy-size unless he set up a trust fund for the child.

Some stories came from the next studio. Or the one next to it.

We were told that Irving Thalberg gave his mother an Hispano Suiza, which she called a Spanish Wheezer.

We were told that at a premiere, Marion Davies broke a priceless string of pearls and exclaimed, "Jeez, me beads!"

We were told that a leading Western star was being castigated by his wife for his heavy drinking, when their maid walked through the room and remarked to the wife, "Well, you've had a snootful yourself."

There were some stories that we had as close as secondhand.

A woman writer fell in love with a performer. He returned her love, but had a wife. The wife, however, signified that she would set him free, for a settlement. The performer happened to be out of funds; the woman writer was not. She made the settlement. The wife kept the money and the husband, too.

A girl made up her mind to get rid of her father's mistress, for her mother's sake. She covered a good many miles to confront the Other Woman—then moved in.

A twelve-year-old, whose mother promised her any guests

she wished for her birthday party, invited a tableful of children her own age, plus the handsome director with whom her mother just then was involved.

And then there were the stories that we *knew*.

Bibi had been offered a commission if she would make all arrangements for a rich woman who had chosen the father she would like for a eugenic child. Bibi didn't feel that kind of agenting was in her line.

Mother's friend Bessie McGaffey, head of a studio research department, took a vacation in the Orient and decided for the sake of business that she ought to visit one of Shanghai's famous brothels. She was stopped at the door, until she improvised that she was a madam from the States. Welcomed at once with open arms, she was shown all the sights (you never know what may be useful in studio research) though she had to draw on all her native wit to make the proper comments displaying properly professional expertise.

We went to dinner again, this time at the Joseph Schildkrauts'. The then Mrs. Joseph Schildkraut, Elise Bartlett, regaled us with an account of her running feud with Rudolph Schildkraut, ex-star of the Yiddish theatre, and her father-in-law. Among other items that annoyed her, he had had a dog she disliked. With an impish smile she described how she had fixed it a nice plate of food—and poisoned it.

My parents just sat there. Maybe they were stunned. Maybe they were sorry for Joseph. Maybe she had poisoned us and we already were too weak to leave? I know I was too weak to leave alone, without a car. The Schildkraut house was on the edge of Laurel Canyon, its woodsy ravines unreached by public transportation even today.

The only real, *old* Hollywood story we knew took place in Laurel Canyon.

Not long after Osmond Borrodaile came back from the war to resume his job as a Lasky cameraman, he and his mother

and his brother Paul were having breakfast in their cottage, when a man drove up the narrow side canyon, left his car, and relieved himself in full view among Mrs. Borrodaile's rock garden flowers. Recognizing the man as a new neighbor, Osmond stepped outside and advised him to go home.

The man replied that he would teach Osmond a thing or two, advanced on him, and pulled out a gun—he was going to blow off Osmond's head! Now aware the man was very drunk, Osmond backed away, but the man advanced. Happily, he stumbled at the porch steps, so Osmond got inside and bolted a screen door. His brother Paul had snatched up their shotgun. Osmond told him not to use it, but that he would get his rifle, which he had to load.

The drunk kicked the screen door. The Borrodaile dog barked. The man fired two shots at her, missed, saw Paul at a window, and drew a bead on him. Paul shoved his gun barrel through the glass, beating him to the draw. He wanted to shoot the gun out of the marauder's hand; the man held the gun to his face, and Paul hit him in the face. Osmond rushed back outside. In spite of the wound, the man still struggled to get a shot at him until subdued by a blow from the butt of his own gun. The police arrived, took Osmond and Paul to the police station, and warned them they would probably be charged with murder—for defending their home? The marauder was in a bad state.

Finally Osmond persuaded his jailers to notify the studio not to expect him on the set. A few minutes later he could hear a policeman at the desk answering the telephone: "Yes, Mr. de Mille...yes...we'll have him there right away." Osmond was hurried to the set.

The marauder recovered after all, and now the sheriff asked Osmond to refrain from pressing charges—though by then this careless neighbor had been identified as a criminal wanted in the East. He had lost an eye and, the sheriff felt, learned his lesson—besides, there was really no room in the county jail.

Shoulder-rubbing, and Other Tales

Even if I didn't want to try my luck walking home from the Schildkrauts and the edge of Laurel Canyon in 1928, surely it was no longer wild as that. So possibly our Hollywood was undergoing change. So possibly I should stop standing still?

Further reflection was postponed. Mother invited me on her vacation.

XXX

Come with Me where Moonbeams

The talkies had arrived—a song here, some chatter there, then a whole play photographed, almost as if still on-stage, a whole score. The equipment at first made acting mobility difficult and actors' voices odd. Then, too, some of the voices which went with the famous faces never were meant to be heard. They were thin, or dull, or nasal, or simply didn't suit the face. Actors "who could speak lines" were rushed from New York. So were writers who could write them. Pictures had a writer—and a dialogue writer; even Mother's pictures. No one stopped to think that she had written plays, with dialogue.

She had just finished a special job on the titles for the *silent* version of *Dynamite*.

She was a good sport about it all, and, besides, she knew the talkies wouldn't last. As soon as the novelty wore off, Lizzie and Jakie would resent this interruption of their privacy inside the theatre. What a nuisance, too, to have to strain your ears for points of plot, above someone's cough! Nice, pithy (silent) titles were far better. Talkies, to Mother, were an early noise pollution. Mrs. Grismer, who had so enlarged our boundaries with Palm Springs, said "Let's go to Honolulu." Mother agreed. Perhaps she thought the talkies might disappear while she was away.

Cecilia had been "to the islands" the previous year and had had a good time—as far as you could guess. Cecilia was la-

Come with Me where Moonbeams

conic. Her dialogue tended towards Noel Coward's "Very large, China; very small, Japan." I was at heart in no hurry to leave California. There was a new, intriguing young man at our beach, where, thanks to Duke Kahanamoku, the Olympic swimmer, we had our captive bit of the islands anyway.

Mother pressed. Anybody who didn't want to travel as far and often as they could Needed Help. I grumbled and gave in, which was fortunate, for the new young man, as it developed, formed his own link with the tropic seas, falling in love with the girl to whom Ramon Novarro sang "The Pagan Love Song" ("Come with me where moonbeams light Tahitian skies") in a charming talkie.

Father refrained from warning us that Honolulu wouldn't be the same as when he visited it back in 1917. (Perhaps he would have warned us, after all, but he had left "for the islands"—in this case the Santa Barbara Islands off our coast—on Uncle Cecil's yacht.)

Mother, Mrs. Grismer, "little" Olive, and I set sail on the *City of Honolulu*. I went below and stayed. I had never been a hardy sailor. On my most recent crossing to Catalina (also on Uncle Cecil's yacht), I barely recovered enough from the one-hour voyage to aquaplane with Katie round the hotel cove, like the characters in *Feet of Clay*. But I was told Mother was superb. She trod the deck like Captain Ahab prior to his wooden leg. The drama of the sea exalted her; salt and spray revived a sense of forbears happier on deck than shore. She had, indeed, a great uncle who went out to Honolulu in 1849.

Uncle Samuel Burbank made the journey for his health and liked it there so well he settled down. He wrote a polite letter back to Maine to send him out his wife. *I am fully aware that it will be unpleasant for you to part with her and the children,* he acknowledged to his father-in-law, *but a woman of her affectionate and generous heart can not be happy so far away from her husband.* He wrote his wife, too, though apparently so serious a matter was decided between the men. He described

the plantation he had bought and the horses he was breaking in ("a black coalt" for little Sammy). His wife was to be sure to bring her saddle. There was no intention, in 1849, of just riding the waves.

All this exuberance on his part hadn't ended in a pineapple or sugar fortune, but in a single spinster of considerable age, our Cousin Mary. At tea on the lanai of the Royal Hawaiian Hotel, looking into a garden that outdid even de Mille sets, Cousin Mary told us in detail just how far Honolulu was from "being the same" and the way it ought to be. The trouble mainly was the tourists. She had little use for them, relatives or not. Fortunately we had done one thing right. We had engaged Duke Kahanamoku's younger brother Sergeant to teach me how to surf. Cousin Mary smiled upon the Kahanamokus. They were pure Hawaiian, and what you had to be was pure. She was pure English-Irish-Scottish (maybe with a dash of Welsh or French) herself.

Like Hollywood Back When, the beach at Waikiki astounded everyone by being small, just a lapful of hotels and bungalows tossed along the sand, and then Diamond Head, which grew on you—and grew and grew. We had done our homework, Earl Derr Biggers' Charlie Chan novel *The Black Camel*, and there was delighted recognition in finding that everything, from the Chinese servant who emptied ashtrays in the hotel lounge to the Stone Wall edging the beach, was as specified.

Mother mostly stayed under our umbrella, close to the Stone Wall, gratefully not needing to find words as she gazed in the direction of Tahiti out beyond the reefs. She did make one excursion in an outrigger, paddling a first-rate oar as all passengers pitched in to catch a wave. She bore no grudge though she came out black and blue, as well as blistered. She concluded we should stay another week! By now this was all right with me. I was beginning to stand up (for several seconds) on a board and to identify the feeling when the board rose on the withers of a wave.

Surfing lessons were at nine. "Little" Olive and I indulged together in the other native art, the hula, but she didn't surf. Her mother felt alarmed by all that coast-to-coast water; after all, Olive was a little younger than I. Sergeant was, too—I think. How could I tell with a young man six feet tall, a cast of feature I had seen only once before (in Duke) and royally black? He was an unbelievable swimmer, of course—all the Stone Wall boys were, native or not—and a splendid teacher. I was only faintly aware (but I was aware) of another, more conventionally handsome teacher, Buster Crabbe, teaching another pupil over in the next batch of waves.

One blue-diamond morning I was on a board, paddling out, overlapped as usual by Sergeant in an intimacy, let alone integration, indispensable and rapidly adjusted to, when we saw a wave was bound to break on top of us.

"Put your head down," Sergeant said.

Had he but said flat! How was he to know my limited and literal mind? So I put my head down. The wave hit me on the back of the neck, and my face bounced on the board. Through the racket of the water I could hear my nose snap. I couldn't feel a thing, but as we surfaced through the foam I must have been a gaudy sight. Blood flows so freely from the face. Sergeant seemed rather pale.

I brushed away some blood and wondered what to do about my shoulder straps. They buttoned and both buttons had just vanished in the foam. Sergeant mentioned heading in. My mind mainly on the buttons, I concurred. I was not at that stage of expertise where I could use both my hands to hold up my shoulder straps while surfing. We zigzagged in, an ocean slalom the teachers did with us as a reward, through the uprights of the jetty near the Outrigger Club, and on the sand we separated. Sergeant's headquarters were at the Club, mine were farther up the beach.

My walk to the Stone Wall was sedate. My nosebleed now had stopped after turning the water only slightly pink for a few miles. I risked a wave at Mother (watch that strap!),

head held high, and shouted that I was going to our room to change.

When I reached the room, I sat down quickly on the bathroom tiles. Not that I was faint, just that I had no real wish to meet a mirror face to face. Polynesian features with broad noses looked magnificent on the Kahanamokus. It seemed unlikely that one would do much for me. All those complaints I had made to myself about my face! (Why wasn't I Garbo? Colleen Moore?) I disavowed them now. Let me just be me.

Finally, as it grew boring sitting on the floor, I got up again. *Let's face it*, I thought, then decided the expression was unfortunate. I had a look. Same old face.

It was different by next morning. My nose swelled into an oblong. Forced to breathe through my mouth, I couldn't smell the sumptuous carnation lei Mother bought me out of sympathy. As to my eyes, they were as dark as Sergeant's skin, though in due course they changed to purple, green, and, at last, a sickly gold. He, I am certain, suffered far, far more than I. The gibes from the Stone Wall, even in Hawaiian, came through loud and clear. *Give 'em hell, Sergeant! What were you doing out there, Sergeant? What is your secret for instructing in the wonders of the waves?*

We suspended lessons for a couple of days, till I was sure my nose would not fall off and (I think) Sergeant got his nerve back. (Was there no end to the folly of *wahinis* and of *malahinis!*) In the interval I learned to play Piute with the Stone Wall boys. They were full-time swimmers, part-time teachers, Anglo-Saxon, Hawaiian, Japanese, Portuguese, or different blends; and they had a lurid reputation, being young, muscular, good-looking, and available—in different blends. I thought they were wonderful: they were my trip to Big Bear with the crew. Besides, Piute was the nicest card game I ever played, though everybody cheated some. There couldn't be a better way to break a nose.

Fortunately I was presentable enough to go with Cousin

Mary and Mother to a reception honoring Hawaii's new governor. I had done no homework on politics and what I noticed principally was the night-blooming cereus. I could smell again.

We prepared to part from Waikiki with poignant regret. I was able to stand up and fall off surfboards pretty well on my own, which I didn't expect would be of much use to me at home. It was then held that you couldn't surf off the California coast, a belief hundreds, if not thousands, of surfers now daily contradict. So I was particularly sorry not to get one last lesson on the day we sailed. Sergeant hadn't thought I'd get up early enough. I did.

It was so early that the beach was bare and at last looked large. The only other wave-watcher was Buster Crabbe. He seemed to have the warmth and kindliness of the Hawaiians by blood, though he was merely Hawaiian-born. He would have managed to take me out surfing this early, he declared, if he had known. Courtesy of the islands.

At noon the *City of Los Angeles*—the other Los Angeles–to–Honolulu ship—moved us past Waikiki. (Very small again, Waikiki.) Everybody threw their farewell leis overboard at Diamond Head because of the superstition that otherwise you never would come back. I saved a gardenia, though, and as California had strict agricultural rules against bringing flowers or fruit ashore, I rolled it in my hair. I had been growing my hair—tackily—for five years. It was worth it, now.

Mrs. Grismer and Olive brought back two macaws. They were named Kamehameha and Liliuokalani, for the famous island rulers. Kamehameha, who was red, was a decent citizen, but Lili, who was blue, was a beast. She bit everyone. Finally she escaped in Laughlin Park. Someone advertised the finding of a splendid blue bird. Mrs. Grismer did not respond. She feared it was a ruse—that Lili had wreaked havoc and she would be sued.

A certain amount of havoc certainly was wreaked that fall. Mother made a note of it. She kept a fact journal, four

lines every day—work, the weather, dinner guests. You did not entrust your *feelings* to a journal, Mother said, in case it should fall into a stranger's hands; you kept it impersonal. *Big cataclysm in the stock market,* she set down in October, 1929. It was a fact, and impersonal—way off there in New York.

She was busy finishing her term at Fox, on Writers' Row, where the paths between the offices and flowerbeds were labeled "Bond Street" or "Rue de la Paix." Father, having come to the conclusion that Los Angeles had grown as far as it could, commuted to Arizona about cotton land.

XXXI
Parties II

I came back from Honolulu deeply infatuated with the islands, but they didn't seem to be really meant for me, any more than Joe had been. Tucking one gardenia in my chignon hadn't proved I was the type for a lifetime of flowers in my hair. I went back to see what friends I still had left at school and show them my tan.

What else was I doing?

Well, since Life in the Islands, I swam sixty laps of Patty Lighton's pool without stopping.

I drove Mother to work.

I drove Mother home from work.

I had had another chance to act. Rupert Julian, a director who became a friend on discovering that Mother was co-author of *The Breed of the Treshams* in which he had toured while still an actor himself, invited me to be in the Wild Party in a picture he was directing (Mother's script) about Flaming Youth. I consulted Mother. She was not opposed. However, some other girl might really *need* the job. Besides, suppose Rupert told me to come out of an alcove pulling down my skirt? Would I want my one adult appearance on film to be so—well—tawdry?

I thanked Rupert and said no, not in fear of being tawdry, but in fear of Junior It Girl Sue Carol, who was his star. When we had been introduced, she looked right over my head,

though she was shorter than I. I took this as a sign that if I came out of an alcove pulling down my skirt, Sue Carol (and the world at large) would suppose I'd snagged it on a chair.

I was not prepared to tell my school friends this. What more was there to tell?

I was almost the best woman volleyball player at the Beach Club.

I was captain of the Hollywood Athletic Club women's volleyball team. As a bonus for that four-year-old hairline fracture of the heart, Joe's wife, Constance Garland Harper, also was on the team; she played very well.

I was author of two book-length manuscripts. One was a romance in the style (I hoped) of Dumas, père. The other was modern, but still arch. I did not refer to them. What my friends at school were dying to know about, as they toasted slimming Ry-Krisp on the high school radiators, were the *parties,* the parties which you had thought would be so much better when you got to high school, and then thought would be so much better afterwards!

In my two free years I had not forgotten high school and its disappointment: social triumph wasn't automatic—no one *ever* handed you a man. In H.S.G.'s high school there was no provision for finding men at all. The school had one official dance a year, the Prom, but no device such as, say, a contact with a local boys' school, for ensuring anything but girl dancers on the floor. You went brush-popping your escort on your own.

Among my senior classmates, the older girls had no trouble. For them school already seemed a mere recess between dates. Those of us who were younger, and not Harleans, sometimes got lost in the brush. A visiting de Mille cousin was my escort at my Prom. I don't suppose he had much of a time—but I did. That year the Prom was held at our house. It was the house the class had requisitioned, and not me; I wasn't even one of the hostesses. But the other escorts thought I was. Everybody danced with me.

Parties II

Theodore Roberts, villain of *The Cost of Hatred*, once said of Mother at her most prolific that the studio should be rechristened Flebbe-Paramount. Not tactful, but nice. Now our school dance was a Flebbe dance. I danced so hard I fell asleep at the clandestine party afterwards. (Because it was forbidden by the school, there always *had* to be another party, after midnight and the finish of the Prom.) At least I was there.

I was there. Those were still key words. They meant something to talk about next day, if not always truthfully. Getting through the Prom with an adequate young man didn't mean the end of cruel tests. There was New Year's. You had to be there—somewhere—at New Year's, with someone, or forevermore lose face.

Father once stepped out of character and invited a young man for me. The young man had shown up with a letter of introduction and a wish to act. He acted well enough so that while accepting the invitation, he brought his own girl, and Father even lent him money—to get *her* a corsage. Sometimes I wondered what it would be like living in West Newbury....

However, there were good New Year's parties, too. John de Mille gave one. When the clock struck twelve I was dancing with Patty's escort, Johnny Weissmuller, so I was the first girl Tarzan kissed in 1929. It was not a statistic that would fit in the Alumnae Notes of the H.S.G. yearbook along with *Julanne Johnston '18, leading woman in Douglas Fairbank's* Thief of Bagdad; *Nancy Adams '22, graduated from The Branch; Lillian Gilmore '26—leads in* Frontier Courage *and* The Phantom Flyer. But it made a point to my friends at school.

That fall season after Honolulu, a future Ape Man briefly loomed for me, too, when Buster Crabbe, whose profile had remained in my mind's eye right along with Diamond Head, came to college in Los Angeles. I knew the family with whom he stayed; Duke Kahanamoku lived there. It was a household full of students, athletes, and keen interests. Both the sons, Tom and Bill Henry, were in training to act.

Buster Crabbe as yet was known entirely for swimming,

but, I rightly guessed, he might want to act, so I asked him to a party at the "new" William de Milles'. Contacts, and all that. He politely refused. He had just got engaged to that other pupil from that other batch of waves.

Still, it was an entertaining party, with a lot of lively people whom—even if you didn't like them all—you were unlikely to forget. A likable person was the actor Ivan Lebedeff. For ten years White Russians (White in the political and not the geographic sense) had been arriving in Hollywood. The stories of their loss of kindred, land, and fortune (they *never* lost their titles) were diverse and harrowing.

Lebedeff had worked in numerous de Mille pictures; his almost Oriental good looks and the pathos of his flight from the Bolsheviks, who killed his horse, had moved me to tears back at De Mille Studio. I found them both a little studied now, but how lovely to be noticed by him, where two years ago he had looked around me as if I were nursery furniture! Could it have been my dark blue taffeta dress with zigzag hem and plunging décolletage? He asked me to his apartment. Frances Beranger was disturbed. She thought I might go.

Into that alcove?

The dark blue dress plainly had less effect on a blonde young man with cornflower blue eyes who sat in one of the William de Mille playroom's few chairs. He'd gladly fetch me a chair if there were another, he remarked as I happened by, but he could not surrender his—he'd had a hard day on the set. I was baffled and curious. Almost everyone I knew had a hard day on the set, but they seldom couldn't stand when they came home. Perhaps this weary victim was a stunt man? He was John Farrow, at that time a writer, later a director, husband of Maureen O'Sullivan, and father of Mia Farrow. I left him to the chair and had a talk with another young man who wrote—I had no idea what. He was so amusing that next day I got his book—*Face Value*, by James Campbell. It was about a young man who grew up in a French bordello. This was less and less like being nursery furniture.

Parties II

There was still a lot of nursery in my heart. I missed costume parties, and perhaps so did my friend Isabelle, who was no longer quite so shy as in the days of Charlie Chaplin's slow-motion kiss. She gave a costume party for Halloween. It was handsomely trimmed with males—a studio had just imported the best-looking youths from a dozen colleges for a movie to be titled *Varsity*.

From Princeton, where little Billy Buckland—now six feet tall—was in his first year, we had Phillips Holmes. He was extraordinarily handsome, full of acting promise. As the son of a successful light comedian, Taylor Holmes, he seemed destined for the movies anyway, without any need to be "discovered" in a college. I spent part of the evening sitting on his lap, not romantically, but because (again) there were few chairs. I was sitting there when another collegian crawled through an archway looking for a pin just as a girl aimed a bucket of water at a lantern catching fire overhead. The water drenched him.

I was living *The Collegians*, the most popular film series of the time! I was in! My girl friends, ones like Katie and Patty who always had a man to take them anywhere, voiced a cautious optimism. Now if only I would get paired off, so they could include me in their parties without second thought. . . .

It happened—a young man at the beach. He had admired me playing volleyball. (Not the playing, we hoped.) He *wanted* to meet me, he *wanted* to take me to Katie's treasure hunt. He was good-looking and—we didn't say peppy so much any more—fun. I helped Katie hide most of the treasure hunt clues. One was in the ear of a life-size plaster elephant which had been erected as an advertisement for a stationery firm halfway to the beach. It was my high point for the party.

Bob called for me late and blew a summoning horn. Father almost didn't let me go. What sort of manners was that? Following the clues, which I enjoyed much more than Bob did, led us to the beach. Katie had food and music ready at the Club. Bob felt that first we ought to step outside. I was less

sophisticated than either one of us had thought. We came quickly in again. Poor Bob! He was already pledged to me for the next event, Patty's birthday dance. Short of suicide, I could think of no way to stay home. As a rule, Father felt about parties the way Mother felt about traveling.

We arrived at Patty's Beverly Hills house on a beautiful warm night in our private temperature of thirty-five degrees. From the garden flashed a neon sign—neon still was new—"*Chez* Pat." A dance floor had been laid across the grass. There was happy splashing in the pool. Perfect Hollywood ingredients! Bob went straight into the house and, I was later told, upstairs to the bar, where he tried to match drinks with William Powell. I doubt if Bob won the match, but I don't know. I never saw him again.

There was plenty to do—swim, meet Charlie Farrell and Virginia Valli, and Stuart Erwin and June Collyer, two permanent and to-be-married pairs, dance with "Big Boy" Williams, veteran of Westerns and rowdy comedy and who for a change of pace would become Fanny Brice's leading man in *My Man*. A beau of Cecilia's drove me home.

That was the year Cecilia reached twenty-one. Uncle Cecil gave her twenty-one bonds, held together with a set of seed pearl jewelry from the Paradise tray—and she got married. Her bridegroom was Frank Calvin, charming, but old, and whom we all knew at the beach. He was *thirty*. His sarcasm could be as sharp as Uncle Cecil's and it was hilarious. On the wedding day we had rain, but otherwise this was a smooth de Mille production till the end when, with the huge reception over, Uncle Cecil took Father aside to share the bottle of champagne he had put down at Cecilia's birth. The champagne was flat.

Most of this going out was fun; much of it meant mingling with stars. But what about the truly "Hollywood" parties, the kind we told the folks back East (who didn't believe it) that we never had? Was I never to see anyone play strip poker, or a

Parties II

couple vanish through a softly closing door, or enlaced beneath a piano? Shouldn't I experience an all-night session, tasting strange drinks, hearing strange jokes, and suspecting strange patterns of romance?

I began to wonder if there might be something really wrong with a young female resident of Hollywood whose wildest orgy was six sets of tennis at Zuma Beach (not even Malibu), followed by a grunion hunt in honor of the famous Amos and Andy, black-face comedians, and a fleeting embrace from a middle-aged British leading man. I liked tennis all right and could get to sleep at nine. Just the same I longed for the option of a bacchanal or at least of a fling.

At this point Agnes de Mille gave a dance recital. To some people she was still just a de Mille, little more than amateur. I was thrilled by the vignettes she performed, from the stories they told and the clothes she designed to her own dancing style. No one ever called her a Pavlova. But how she could project!

After the recital we all gathered at the House. It was such a happy night, what a shame it couldn't just go on and on! Douglass Montgomery, home from New York, seemed to feel that way. He invited everybody for a moonlight swim. Moonlight swim! Even if he lived in Altadena, and not Hollywood, surely this was Hollywood at last!

We set out in a small fleet of cars, among them one with Ramon Novarro and a friend from the East, and one with me and Isabelle and her recent bridegroom. Since Bob, there had been less friendly pressure to make me into a pair.

Doug's house was in the foothills, with a lot of lawn where Agnes danced again, until she tripped against a faucet. There was indeed a moon, and we swam. Mostly I swam. The pool was cold. Gradually car by car drove away. I still swam. Better the cold in the pool than the cold of getting out. Finally, towards the desert, the sky started getting light. My parents knew where I had gone. They never worried much. Still, it

would be nice for me to be at home in bed before they went to work. Isabelle had left. I looked round for another ride.

I wish I could record that Ramon Novarro, truly a great star whether you preferred him in *Ben Hur* or (as Mother did) in *The Red Lily* and *Where the Pavement Ends*, volunteered to drive me home. He didn't, but he did the next best thing. Wanting to stay on for breakfast himself, he asked his friend from the East, who had an early business engagement, to look after me.

It was a very silent drive.

No matter—very little matter. We took a wrong turn and went by the Green Hotel, softened in every tile and arch by dawn. In the car with its top down, looking back from the Pasadena Bridge, I could watch the sunrise reach to the last pad of snow on Mt. Baldy and the dots of yucca on Mt. Hollywood. Dew caught fire on some scattered orange trees, a few geraniums. We crossed the railroad tracks at what no one by then called Tropico—it was a part of Glendale. We passed the house Bibi once mistook for Uncle Cecil's. We swung into Laughlin Park.

I was in bed at half-past five, tired, satisfied, of course—and a little hollow, too. I had had my Hollywood party. The hollowness no doubt was due to lack of food.

XXXII
Leaving

After *Their Own Desire* Mother was satisfied that she still could write a book. She had left for the islands feeling no one but Mill realized how well she could write for pictures. She came back refreshed, ready to follow him to RKO, where he was a supervisor. Supervisor was the name given then to the on-the-set producer—the one responsible for real production of a picture, often of several pictures at the same time—not the man engaged in higher studio policy upstairs.

Talkies had not disappeared, but for Mill she wrote dialogue. He was aware of her abilities. The fact that even now relatively few people were remained in part her fault, for rejecting publicity. But *look* at publicity—*The King of Kings* was based on the Gospels, yet a Broadway marquee of tremendous size proclaimed, "*The King of Kings*—story by Jeanie Macpherson." And even if now she saw some sense in advertising, what was there to say—"Since 1916 Beulah Marie Dix has had her name on more than thirty scripts?" That would have sounded old and perhaps outworn.

The other reason for her almost-anonymity was the scripts on which she had worked but which *didn't* have her name. She did a lot of helping out and doctoring and, until 1936 when the Screen Writers' Guild achieved some rights, writing-credits on films got awarded somewhat haphazardly. While writers had had less things to do (no more filling in as script clerk or film

editor), they had more people to write with, the supervisor for one, and then—as the philosophy grew that two or three pens must be better than one—various collaborators. Sometimes the product was successful; mostly it was synthetic; as to where the credit went—that could depend on studio goodwill, nepotism, or the wise aggression of the writer. Mother had a minimum of wise aggression.

Still, she was at work—and still work was a holy word. How then could it happen that as I stood round hollowly, she didn't urge it upon me? Because, I think, she didn't know what work to urge. She had passed the point where writing was the only work, at least for someone near to her. She had reached the point where she would not have wanted her worst enemy to work in motion pictures, if that enemy was a creative one. Why did *she* go on? She was accustomed; there were compensations with Mill, through his sensitivity and wit. Sound Could Even Be Fun—they enjoyed inventing a player-piano alibi for the killer in their first R.K.O. suspense picture.

But she wanted more for me. Or perhaps in her heart she agreed with Father, whose attitude was like the one he took about me and the actors. He couldn't think of any work good enough for me, or any I was good enough to do. Well, I had a few years left. I was nineteen. *Someday* I would work—it seemed as far away as being forty. Fortunately, while we were not really rich ("Hollywood people are crazy," Mother used to say, "they treat salary like income"—and then she herself treated salary like income), there was no financial necessity.

We talked a little about my going on in school. Mother thought that Radcliffe had let her down—no more of that free-elective system she so happily recalled. If I had to face a lot of science and math, why go all the way back East? Why go through a drab four years? I wasn't likely to teach. I wouldn't, she supposed, use my degree otherwise. I could *read* at home. I did read, mainly *Dracula*, in our sunroom, snacking toast and cheese, and French. I never had much use for knowledge

Leaving

about vampires in Transylvania but I got a lot out of the French.

When she was at home on week ends, Mother sat behind a wrought-iron grille in her downstairs library, sketching at a play about possessive motherhood, while I went to tennis. More and more I played tennis at the Turnbulls'. Right after Blanche Lasky Goldwyn married Hector Turnbull, the World War I correspondent and author of *The Cheat*, they built a house near the Laskys'. It became famous for the fact that "Aunt" Blanche asked the architect to include a coat closet in the downstairs hall, and he did—a closet for *a* coat. Now the Turnbulls had moved to an Elizabethan manor in West Hollywood with hedges, tennis court, croquet lawn, and presumably more closet space.

Ruth Lasky Goldwyn Turnbull was a happy stepdaughter and I was a happy guest. We had tennis foursomes with a tall, heavy youth from next door, who not only became thin, but the European head of MGM and with Mischa Auer, a born clown who would soon find his own special niche in films. After we had all been to an opening one night, he found a niche on top of a mammoth ashstand in the lobby of the Roosevelt Hotel where he pretended that he was a gargoyle.

I had new friends. One was Virginia Volland. She had great talent for design—we designed pajamas together, to be made up in Hong Kong, but somehow the designs never did get mailed—and she wanted to act. Her mother, it appeared, had been a beauty, and on meeting her mother's friends when she was small, Virginia had heard, "Well, no one will ever be as beautiful as Gladys." Virginia grew up with a firm ambition to be beautiful as Gladys. So she had to act. If you acted, you were beautiful.

Another new friend, Janet Riesenfeld, had been born unmarred by doubt. My New England mother and German father hatched a games player in me. Janet's New England mother and Austrian father (a musical conductor and composer of

movie scores) hatched a Spanish dancer in her. We implored her to dance for us and were disappointed—as she had known—when she demonstrated heeltaps. Our idea of Spanish dancing was a lot of swirling with a shawl.

A message came from an old friend. Margaret de Mille wrote from the East to be sure to look up her theatrical colleague Dorothy Burgess who was touring in *The Squall.* Katie and I hurried to the play and called backstage. Dorothy Burgess seemed depressed that neither one of us was the girl with the name that sounded most thoroughly de Mille, Cecilia.

I went to other plays, I went to movies, I went out at night, I wrote a short story about swimming in the Garden of Alla pool, but the best times kept on being at the Turnbulls'. If Hector Turnbull and perhaps Basil Rathbone, the lank actor who loved playing "Romeo" but would be an ideal "Sherlock Holmes," were on the tennis court, Ruth and I would try croquet. She was good at it. The best swings I made usually zeroed on my foot.

One morning she telephoned me to ask if I would like to go to France.

Hollywood was being rather nice—well, okay—but this wasn't the sort of question you answered with a hasty no. The inspiration we all supposed I might be waiting for (or the man who might do just as well) could be over the next net. Or not.

Rather far, France?

Not too far, Mother thought. (Anybody Who Doesn't Want to Travel, etc.) Father, to my surprise, hardly said a thing. He was hardly home; business took him to Arizona more and more.

All at once I knew that this was what I'd wanted all along. Shake off the dust. It doesn't mean you aren't fond of the dust, only that dust clogs the wheels. Over Baked Alaska, particulars for the trip got straightened out. Ruthie was to study painting. I would study what I pleased. We would go our separate ways all day but be under the same roof at night. We would live on parallel allowances.

Leaving

Once while packing I had the grace to wonder what the next months would be like for Mother, minus my companionship, my chauffeuring. She had Father and Mill—she felt she would get by. She was writing on a project called *Creation*, for which marvelous prehistoric monster models had been made. (*Creation* never did get shot and the monsters turned up in *King Kong*.) I was glad to leave her having fun.

On September 4, 1930, news from mainland China was that Chiang Kai-shek was about to put down last traces of rebellion in the north—any claims about a rebel government entrenched in Peiping were absurd! A plot to murder Mussolini was uncovered in Trieste. A hurricane was heading for our southeast coast.

Inside the United States, financial experts said that as the business "low" of 1929 hadn't been as bad as that of 1921 or 1922, the recovery would certainly be quicker, and the recovery of 1922 had required no more than a year.

Polo was a major subject in the sports section of *The Los Angeles Times*. Los Angeles had just become the nation's fifth largest city. There were thirty-eight suits for divorce and one brush fire. My new friend Virginia Volland took part in a pageant. A studio carpenter died in a fall from scaffolding. A snapshot buff suffered a snakebite when he tried to photograph one rattler of what proved to be a pair.

That was the item that most interested me. We had held a farewell picnic in the foothills on September third. After we found the one possible flat site for eating lunch, a snake popped its head from a centrally located hole. Father spread our blanket right across the hole and, at the urging of Aunt Mildred Smith, we sat on the blanket.

September fourth was the day for Ruth and me to start our trip.

On the way to the train Mother got the least bit quavery. "Take care of yourself," she said. I must have looked dismayed, for she hurried to provide a quotation that would steady things.

She chose a favorite of mine, from Beatrix Potter's "Tailor of Gloucester," where the mice who have repaid the kindness of the ailing tailor by embroidering a waistcoat for him leave a note with the one unfinished bit: "No more twist."

"Take care of yourself," Mother went on. "If something happens to you, no more twist."

We got on the train with lots of going-away gifts. As we waved to our friends, all of them—and some of them were *old* and not too beautiful—looked young and beautiful and rich.

XXXIII
Hollywood, France

Air mail went from Los Angeles to New York twice in twenty-four hours, but people went by train, and people you knew took the Chief.

We had two compartments and a drawing room because Aunt Blanche and Hecky Turnbull were going along for a look at the plays. Our connecting doors were open, making our own private vista of berths and an atmosphere suitable for theatre comedy or suspense. The only suspense was in the Turnbulls' efforts to teach me bridge.

In New York, we went directly to the theatre, almost from the train. Hollywood and New York had a love-hate relationship. We needed New York for finance. They needed us for films. We always felt they were just barely on our side. Still, you *had* to look at plays.

There were also the shops, and we had to admit that though Los Angeles plus Hollywood and Beverly Hills offered glorious ones, New York offered more. Aunt Blanche took us out to get our going-away presents from herself and Hecky. What would we like? While I was wondering if a Brownie camera was a greedy wish, she mentioned the sort of gift she had in mind. The Turnbulls were the least ostentatious people in the West. They never gave presents to impress. They never liked receiving them. (I did.) What Aunt Blanche had in mind seemed lavish.

Ruthie remained calm but I bubbled into Cartier and Tiffany. She ended with lapis and I ended with tourmaline. Hecky gave me an old typewriter, too, when he found that Mother, the Brünnhilde of the Barlock, hadn't thought one indispensable for me. Maybe there was underlying meaning in this—a typewriter wasn't a friendly instrument? Maybe Mother felt if I wrote home in longhand she would get more vibrations of my state of mind.

Everybody other than the Turnbulls warned us not to expect Paris to be the same as back in 1923. Flashing my green tourmaline, I crossed the green water with Ruthie, not at all seasick (very large, the *Ile de France*), to the green landscape, where we settled down in Paris, both of us very green.

We selected a pension on the Right Bank, partly because most Americans preferred the Left, partly because we would be on the Left Bank daily anyway, Ruthie at life class and I at the Sorbonne. This way, we would have to get acquainted with Paris on both sides of the Seine. We intended to be all Paris, not in the least Hollywood. We bought black dresses and turquoise blue beads (every French woman we saw wore that combination then) and we had our tawny polo coats dyed black.

Just the same, even if we didn't say a word, we got found out. Our landlord claimed it was because we were taller than most local girls, and could walk better, with our longer legs. French women weren't as athletic then as we were. Only German and Scandinavian women were.

We would end up forced to concede we were from California. It was one of the few sections of the United States the Parisians were aware of and approved—a playland, sunny, rich. We tried never to admit we belonged to Hollywood. Still, there had been an offer from Ruthie's Uncle Jesse Lasky of a pass to Paris Paramount, a leading movie theatre—organ, everything! Ruthie used it a few times so we could impress

Hollywood, France

young men; we got whisked to seats right past a waiting crowd. Angry murmurs rose.

This had happened before, at the Million Dollar Theatre in Los Angeles, when I was small. Mother took me to the daytime premiere of *Treasure Island;* Shirley Mason starred. As special guests, we were admitted to the lobby while a crowd of raging mothers and their young waited on the sidewalk for a delayed opening of doors. I allegedly declaimed, about the hubbub outside, that I felt like Marie Antoinette at the storming of the Tuileries.

The crowd in Paris wasn't quite so raging. However, it included the type of citizen that actually did storm the Tuileries and though you weren't *scared*—not being Marie Antoinette—it was disquieting.

Another nostalgic touch was that we dropped in on Auntie Bessie Lasky, a bit of Hollywood away from home. She was staying at the newest, glossiest hotel, the *Georges Cinq* and patronizing art as well as studying with an artist. She received us one forenoon at the nearest thing to a levee in my experience. She was in bed in heaps of chiffon and lace. When she finally got up, I discovered she had painted toenails. I was shocked. I had come to Paris for my first painted toenails!

A few weeks later we, too, went to hell and, on the top floor of a hotel at Mont St. Michel, with a moonlit view of the Abbaye from our bedroom window, we plucked our eyebrows for the initial time.

Auntie Bessie took us to lunch at the Ritz and to galleries where we examined Kieslings, our first contact with the paintings with the black eyes that followed you. She bought us tickets for the current stage hit, *Le Sexe Faible.* Talking on the telephone to Mill's sister, who had married a French general, I referred to the play as "La *Sexe Faible"* and she reproved me with what I considered Gallic wit. "In France," she said, "you will find out that sex is always masculine."

Not long after this, Auntie Bessie left. Uncle Jesse, it ap-

peared, had use for the letter of credit with which she was traveling. *Our* money arrived steadily, and steadily I went to an early morning class about Charlemagne and his flowing beard, given by a professor with a flowing beard. In the afternoon I visited museums and often in the evenings joined Ruthie and her new friend Mac at a sketch class. We had a letter of introduction to sculptor Jo Davidson, prominent expatriate, and he gave us excellent advice: "It's a great life, if you weaken." We were rather sedate and thought him flip.

We had a letter also, thanks to Mother's shoulder-rubbing, to the famous Gertrude Stein. We were invited to an evening at the Rue de Fleurus. I began inauspiciously by mistaking Alice B. Toklas for Gertrude Stein. (I didn't quite believe there was anybody named Alice B. Toklas.) Then we walked round the studio room and stared at strange Picassos, for which we were unprepared. Furthermore, Gertrude Stein had the only dog I ever disliked—and she served warm wine. We had been warned (by a dandy of the Mauve Decade, I believe), to beware of warm wine, whose flavor could conceal a drug. Gertrude Stein, white slaver? She couldn't have been nicer, in a brusque way, to a couple of teenage Philistines. How pretty the red wine in a white glass; what a pity we were *not* prepared!

We went to Barbizon, where such a lot of painters had been, and to the homes of Balzac and Hugo, in case they might inspire me, and to the Ile St. Louis, which would inspire anybody. An acquaintance of Father's lived there in romantic, gloomy rooms. She had been a Hollywood publicist and still kept up communication. Thanks to her we had the unforgettable experience of hearing a Goldwyn told a Goldwyn joke. (In those days a lot of useful misuse of the English language was attributed to Samuel Goldwyn, such as the phrase "include me out.") Our friend, of course, was unaware that Ruth was Goldwyn's daughter, and I think quite often so was Ruth. The joke had no more sting for her than if it had concerned Uncle Cecil or Charlie Chaplin.

Hollywood, France

In spite of reminders we spent hours when Hollywood seemed very far away, and would react with a start if because of our accent or our legs someone queried us about it. Our French friends idolized Charlie Chaplin. They were conscious of de Mille. But didn't we know Garbo? Then we must be imposters.

However, what they cared about most of all that year we lived in Paris was the MacDonald affair.

Jeanette MacDonald had become a very big star in Ernst Lubitsch musicals, with her pretty face and voice and the kind of coquetry (still known as "naughty but nice") which began to disappear along with vamps and breach-of-promise suits.

What was that about Jeanette MacDonald? we asked. We hadn't heard a thing.

Our new friends shook their heads. Now we must be *pretending* ignorance. Everyone had heard. This was gospel: Jeanette MacDonald was in the South of France recovering from injuries to that pretty face. We said we doubted it. Oh, yes, they went right on, there was no question here—the question was in how the injuries occurred. One story, and the story they hoped we would confirm, was that Prince Umberto of Italy had told Princess Marie-Jose of Belgium on their wedding night that theirs could be no more than a marriage of state, his heart was given to the American. So, at the earliest occasion, Princess Marie-Jose had at the American.

We never found a whit of substantiation to this tale, which would have made a good plot for a Lubitsch black musical. We never even found that Jeanette MacDonald was in France. But our friends didn't give up. They stuck to the thought that we weren't talking, though they did begin to fear from our blank looks mixed with outrage that we might be morons, sent away for decent burial in foreign student life.

I was crazy about Paris, even if it wasn't—quite—the same as when I glimpsed it in 1923, nor, of course, as before World War I, the Franco-Prussian War, the Terror, the Fronde, and the Massacre of St. Bartholomew.

Why would anybody ever leave?

One morning I came back to the pension after a week end at Louveciennes, and the concierge had Mother's usual biweekly letter waiting for me. Only it was not quite usual.

Dear Evelyn, she began, *It is all over.* Ah, those tones across the years from Sarajevo! *We are wiped out. We are packing a few things and will auction off the rest, with the house. Take the first convenient boat and meet us at the farm. We are through with Hollywood.*

Mother typed her letters and her typing, as always, was extremely good. Yet the print seemed to waver now. I spread the paper flat against the wall of the concierge's booth and read the rest, not very much, right to the signature she always used (and her pen with her initials had been firm), *Believe me as always your loving mother, BF.*

XXXIV
S.W.A.K.

Of course we weren't really through with Hollywood.

We were all back, in about a year, after the backwash of my father's bankruptcy. Maybe he had not been the wisest of all possible businessmen. A lot of businessmen hadn't. Mother used to quote wryly the good advice experts frequently offered married women: don't trust your husband blindly. Would she have lived with someone she did not trust blindly?

Father's Arizona land became superbly productive, but not then, and not for us.

My affectionate mother, BF, resumed writing for the screen almost without a break. Her name had not been shouted from the roof tops before; she became entirely anonymous now. Chivalrously, Mill took on all the outside contacts of their partnership. Mother stayed in their secret office, unreachable—a conspiracy between Millhausers and Flebbes somewhat like the attitude we had had towards Bibi's Perch. Mother felt that auctioning off your house was like being seen in public in your underclothes. She had no wish to be on view, even fully clothed, after that.

We went back to Hollywood—but never to *our* Hollywood, for Hollywood was not the same. Perhaps it hadn't been for quite a while, but without the perspective of absence, and a little agony, we hadn't realized it. Talkies were there to stay, and the Depression had a very fixed air, too.

The entertainment industry went on. In those glum days, entertainment was something people had to have, cheaper than food, tidier than suicide. Even so, there wasn't movie work enough to go round. Actors no longer lolled along the Boulevard, staring in store windows at their own reflections. They were hunting jobs, No Experience Needed, or working for the WPA, which put on fine plays—*Meet the People*, a black *Mikado*, and an even more delightful, though less acclaimed, black *Fra Diavolo*.

The oranges grew and the oil pumped, evidently not lucratively. Everybody said the weather was getting worse. The Dinky disappeared, then the Hollywood School for Girls, some of its buildings absorbed into the complex of the new Hollywood Women's Club. Trees died or were cut down, mockingbirds moved out, streets got repaved, new buildings rose—though nothing could rise higher than thirteen stories until after 1956—and it became hard to tell whether the Japanese store and the Women's Exchange used to stand just here or over there. Houses clambered every hill. The 57 sign was gone. There was hardly any smell of sage.

But the taste?

If I closed my eyes, I could still taste the poured velvet of the cocoa Sunday night at the Hollywood Athletic Club, the tangy tomato bisque at the Victor Hugo, and the first bite of the Monte Cristo sandwich at the Beach Club—you had to yawn to get so many layers of turkey, bread, and cheese into your mouth. Then there was the ice-cream cake at Thistle Cottage, on the road to the beach, where Katie and I shared a mound through a minor earthquake. Still further back, there was that first chocolate apple, under the Christmas tree at Argyle Avenue, an apple of the knowledge that the world was good—the rocks might bruise, not break, the mud might smear, not smother, the wind rushed, but it wouldn't blow you down. If it did, you had on your crepe bloomers.

There had been such endless places to go! Up in the al-

S.W.A.K.

mond tree, out to watch Joe Kamemura's quackless ducks, down the hill in the kiddie car my mother hated and feared, and which Poe, Aunt Constance's chauffeur, kindly repaired for me.

In the middle of the night director Melville Brown rushed down from his Vine Street house. Rex Ingram, one of the very best and certainly the handsomest director in Hollywood, had been taken ill. Did we have mustard? Bibi did. The Browns said we saved Rex Ingram's life with our mustard on their plaster.

When we came back to Hollywood, we lived in lower Beverly Hills, but Mrs. Borrodaile's device still worked, for a while. You did not float downstairs now to the living room with always twilit beams, but out under the sky on a cloud as soft as Uncle Cecil's bearskin rug, and you felt as light as the vast blue balls, more like balloons, we had used for dancing Isadora Duncan–style. Just above, the stars gleamed cheerfully—or was that Mother's shoe buckles?

Down below, little Hollywood spread out, the carbarns at Sherman, Magnetic Hill (now gone, the road remade, some county engineer's revenge on illusion), the eucalyptus stands and tousled palms, the canyons and the trails, the studios and stores, the people and the school—all very small, small enough to fit into the heart. Hollywood Boulevard, where some buildings had lawns, and some buildings had false fronts, where the sidewalk offered elbowroom, the policeman waved, the streetcar would wait for you, and the mockingbirds were friends....

That was the way it was.

Wasn't it?

The chord that bound me to the Montessori class twanged loud when the Nazis moved towards Paris, only a few years later on, and a thought was the result: *Last night I dreamed about Paris/As if it were here in the room,/The grey of the rain from the terrace,/The glow of the chestnuts in bloom.*

The second verse explained that everybody said *this* time

Paris never possibly could be the same, and the thought concluded:

Last night I dreamed about Paris/so clearly an artist could draw it./Oh Hera, oh Eros, oh Charis,/Was it ever as anyone saw it?

But so much has been written about Paris. Isn't it Hollywood we mean?

*Last night I dreamed about childhood,
The groves and the lanes and the trolley,
The beach where the old picture sets stood,
The hills with their mustard and holly.
It was Hollywood, Vine Street and Highland
And Sunset, so sharp you could draw it.
Oh magic and movable island,
Was it ever as anyone saw it?*

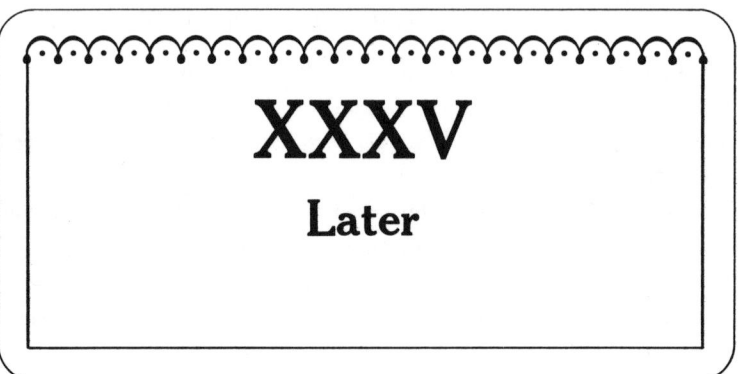

XXXV
Later

Nancy Adams married her half-niece Cecilia's brother-in-law, Bert.

Agnes de Mille went on dancing, choreographed, and then wrote.

Katie de Mille went on being beautiful and married actor Anthony Quinn.

Margaret de Mille became an executive with Elizabeth Arden, whose beauty products could not have been better promoted than by her skin.

Cecilia de Mille and Frank Calvin were divorced.

Constance Garland and Joe Harper were divorced.

Cecilia and Joe were married.

"Little" Olive Grismer, Joe's sister, married Frank Calvin.

Phillips Holmes starred in *An American Tragedy* on the screen; he was very promising; he died in an aircraft training accident in World War II.

Wilfred Buckland, builder of romantic castles, believed his son Billy was incurably ill and killed Billy and himself.

Ramon Novarro, the young shepherd who had danced, was beaten to death in the Laurel Canyon hills.

Virginia Parsons, ex-Indian rider, became an illustrator of children's books. Virginia Volland, would-be actress, became a designer of stage clothes. Ruth Turnbull married McClure Capps, the Mac we knew in Paris, who became a motion-picture set designer.

The thing my parents greatly feared occurred. I went to work in the movie industry and married an actor. Movies boomed through World War II, boggled at television, battered their way on.

Beulah Marie Dix Flebbe died September 25, 1970, in her sleep, at the age of ninety-three. It was the first night of terrible brush fires which swept Southern California with greater devastation than in the days when Paradise burned down.

If she had been aware, she would have agonized for the animals, the children, the old people—even in this case for just the people—who were hurt. But she was not aware.

She didn't know at all that a brush fire was near—unless some subconscious sense of theatre had been reached, to close a curtain for her exactly then or to open one.

——NO MORE TWIST——

About the Author

Evelyn F. Scott was born in Brookline, Massachusetts, and when she was very, very young got to Hollywood via the apron strings of her mother, a successful author and playwright, who was going out "just for a visit," at the home of her friend and colleague, Beatrice de Mille. The visit, though not always at "Bibi" de Mille's, lasted fifty-four years. Mrs. Scott shares the devotion her mother, Beulah Marie Dix Flebbe, developed for motion pictures, and has spent the majority of her working life as a story analyst for various studios. Since 1952 she has been at MGM. Married to a film editor and the mother of a daughter, she is one of the rare few who look forward to Monday morning and another week of work ahead.

She is the author of a book for children, *The Story of the Fourteen Bears*.

APR 1 5 1981

3/6/81

GAYLORD PRINTED IN U.S.A.

791.4309
Sc083h

58795

HOWE LIBRARY
SHENANDOAH COLLEGE &